T0274139

Outside the Outside

Outside the Outside

The New Politics of Suburbs

Matt Hern

VERSO

London • New York

First published by Verso 2024
1 3 5 7 9 10 8 6 4 2

Verso
UK: 6 Meard Street, London W1F 0EG
US: 388 Atlantic Avenue, Brooklyn, NY 11217
versobooks.com

Verso is the imprint of New Left Books

ISBN-13: 978-1-78873-817-0
ISBN-13: 978-1-83976-063-1 (US EBK)
ISBN-13: 978-1-83976-062-4 (UK EBK)

British Library Cataloguing in Publication Data
A catalogue record for this book is available from the British Library

Library of Congress Cataloging-in-Publication Data
A catalog record for this book is available from the Library of Congress

Typeset in Sabon by MJ & N Gavan, Truro, Cornwall
Printed and bound by CPI Group (UK) Ltd, Croydon CR0 4YY

Contents

Part 1

GETTING OUTSIDE

We solve the city problem by leaving the city.

—Henry Ford

1

Today a rare sun of spring. It's not even noon and it's already blistering hot, searing my squinty little eyes. It takes forever to walk anywhere out here: this so-called city is designed to punish pedestrians, and there is no respite from the rising glare. The treeless, desiccated blocks are miles long. The traffic is everywhere. There's nothing to look at but low-end big boxes. I'm flustered, vaguely panicky, scanning the horizon for any kind of shade.

Okay, fine, it's not actually *that* bad. I'm getting a little theatrical here as the day heats up and I work my way across this parched lakebed of a parking lot, but the heat really has started to broil me.

I am in Surrey. Vancouver, BC's biggest suburb.

Surrey should be called a city. It has almost six hundred thousand people in it, just a little less than the population of the City of Vancouver, but like so many suburban communities on the fringes of big cities, it is growing so fast it will soon surpass its metropole in population. Surrey has doubled in official population in the past twenty-five years and sprints to inhale people as fast as it can.

That's probably not all of it. I am confident that Surrey is actually far more populous than Vancouver already: this is a city of migrants, a city with a large majority "visible minority" population. A city full of people who have few reasons to trust government officials. People who definitely won't be answering unexpected phone calls or knocks on the door asking about how many individuals live in their household.

But despite all the size and growth and energy here, this doesn't look or feel like a big city. Or really, even a city at all.

Surrey sits on a giant physical footprint and people are spread thin. First built on once-fertile agricultural land rolling out toward the Fraser Valley, it has had little reason to constrict sprawl, and so sprawl it has. Like any good suburb, the municipal regulatory architecture has placed few restrictions on major development. Desperate for investment, Surrey frantically courts capital and urban planners green-light every half-witted proposal, so now it is an immense jumble of metastasizing low-density housing tracts punctured with transit-proximate towers, mismatched shopping malls, mini-malls, and strip malls. There's no real downtown, no cohesive urban planning, nowhere to walk, and traffic. So much traffic.

Surrey is a classic North American suburb. You know this place. You've been here. Grown up here. Sneered at it. Used it as the butt of jokes. You've done everything you can to put distance between yourself and the goddamn wastelands.

Suburbs are deployed as a proxy for every ill that besets the contemporary built landscape. A synonym for "deplorable urban development." Geographies of nowhere. Ecological catastrophes. Cultural sinkholes. Shorthand for ugliness and banality and homogeneity and anomie. Everyone who writes, or sings, or films suburbs wants to mock or discipline or fix or bomb them. Suburbs have been called "the greatest misallocation of resources the world has ever known" and much worse.[1]

Suburbs are awful. The absolute worst. And yet, here I am. What am I doing?

2

At the beginning, I had no idea. When I first began spending time in Surrey, I had only the most embarrassingly ill-formed notions about what I was looking for or how to conduct myself.

But I knew I had to be here. All across the globe, poor and working-class residents are being expelled from inner cities. I knew for certain that I needed to start thinking way more seriously about the edges of cities, but had few ideas about what that kind of project looked like. I felt boxed in by my own sureties: all my theorizing about cities left me constantly angry and disappointed. I was dismayed at where decades of urban organizing had left me.

Vancouver's much-celebrated urban planning achievement—inner-city density, walkable neighborhoods, transit-proximate development, and so on—has rendered just another banal city that looks and feels like so many others in the Global North. Vancouver is awash in the same frantic courting of capital, the same relentless displacement of residents by condoization and speculations, the same dumb-ass "smart city" clichés, the same spectacularist touristic forays, the same housing market brutality, the same tiresome liberal handwringing.

Inner cities everywhere are being emptied of community and affordability by market surges and housing portfolio expansionism, enabled by a bourgeois urbanism that fetishizes bike lanes and craft beer, coffee shops and farmers' markets, sustainable development and smugness as the apex of urban life. It is a trajectory that the pandemic did not cause, only accelerated. People would not be pouring out of cities, rushing to telecommute from new, distant locales if they loved where they lived, if their cities were vibrant, welcoming, safe and affordable. The urban land market creates a gross paradox: the more conventionally attractive cities are, the faster they are cleansed of low-income and working residents, leaving behind only cold-hearted xenophobia, flailing faith in market-produced supply, and whitewashed bourgeois density. Commentators who want to blame Covid for barren city streets and empty office towers are willfully missing the forest for the trees.

Perhaps that sounds a little overwrought. I tend to be in a grim mood these days when I think about Vancouver and so many other cities that I know and love. There are still wonderful pockets in every city, still all kinds of vibrancy, still fight in every dog, still all kinds of hopefulness. But mostly, decent people are leaving inner cities, trying to get out before they are entirely overrun: they are moving to smaller towns, they find some random neighborhood somewhere, they luck into co-op or subsidized housing, they head out to distant semi-rural commutes, they work from home, they quit. More than anything, though, people are moving to the suburbs.

The immense population growth here in Surrey is hardly unique: in cities everywhere, surplus, "less-productive" residents are being reordered further and further away on the margins of metropolitan regions. When I was young, the term *inner-city neighborhood* was code for Black, immigrant, and poor. To my kids, *inner-city* means high-end condo-ization, gentrification and tourist-oriented, sanitized shopping districts.

I used to live in one of those inner-city neighborhoods. I spent all of my adult life in East Vancouver, running local non-profits and doing community organizing for decades with low-income kids and families. My family rented in a central neighborhood that was historically the urban landing spot for Indigenous people, newcomers, working-class families, and everyone who needed cheap shelter. The Eastside was always, in the indelicate words of a friend, the "dumping ground" for the rest of the city. But starting in the mid-nineties, that started changing, and swiftly. As my pal put it, "Matt, you need to get out to the suburbs. The people you work with aren't in East Vancouver anymore. They're in Surrey."

6

I resisted hard, but he was—and is—right. The East Vancouver that I knew and loved, the Commercial Drive where I raised my family, has transformed. Like so many inner-city neighborhoods, so many of its modestly incomed residents have been replaced, and those that have found ways to stay are buffeted by astoundingly brazen rent gouging.

Twenty years ago, when a young single mother would show up at our door, interested in one of the programs I ran, one of the first questions I would ask is where she lived. And the answer was always in one of the nearby neighborhoods: the Drive, Mount Pleasant, Strathcona, the Downtown Eastside. Now, though, when I get an email with that question, they live in a place I have barely heard of and probably never been to. It's a twenty-minute bus ride to the Brentwood Mall. It's a half-hour walk to the Willowbrook Shopping Centre. It's in some suburban zone that doesn't even really have a name and I have to look up.

This is not much of a surprise to anyone. As gentrification continues to ravage Vancouver as it does pretty much every other city, our old neighborhood remains among the most vulnerable. Close to the downtown core, with some preserved housing stock, a walkable high street, good public transit and a vibrant, "edgy" reputation, the neighborhood has been rapidly corroded by voracious capital, rising rents, property speculation and a wave of swanky craft beer bars, cafés, toy stores and weird hipster places no one I know goes into.

Inner-city communities are not helpless victims: their transformations remain uneven, halting, fraught and resisted. But the plight of our old neighborhood will be immediately recognizable to most any urban dweller. Seemingly in a flash, it became exclusive: wealthier, blander, more predictable, and a whole lot whiter.[2]

In city after city across the globe, these ongoing cycles of displacement have become so chronic that ritualistic cleansings of local residents, businesses, and community ventures are now expected, normalized as just the everyday workings of the urban marketplace. We are all inured to it, numbed by the losses around us—our friends, families and neighbors pushed out of the neighborhood, family businesses closing, buildings torn down and replaced with something made of glass and brushed steel. Any attractive community in any city is exposed, and especially if they are close to the urban core.

It's trite to point out that modestly incomed people can rarely afford to live close to downtown anymore. These new forms of spatial precarity have moved past cliché into orthodox urbanism. And it is not all that new: as the *Nation* documented as early as 2007, "For the first time ever, more poor Americans live in the suburbs than in all our cities combined."[3]

We are living in the midst of an exhaustively documented, historic—and historically dislocating—global rush to cities. Agile real estate, developer and marketing interests, in collaboration with new occupying forms of capital—encouraged and greased by putatively progressive urban planners—are reclaiming the city with startling ferocity.

The sheer speed of this urban occupation is aggressively forcing poorer residents out of city cores to areas where physical isolation exacerbates social marginalization. In cities from Seattle to Seoul to Sofia and everywhere in between, poor, middle- and working-class people are finding it increasingly difficult to find viable housing, jobs and commercial opportunities in premium inner-city neighborhoods. It is not happening at the same velocity or in the same pattern everywhere—every city evinces its own peculiarities and tendencies—but in cities across the planet, a startling phenomenon is unfolding. It is something people sense immediately and anecdotally observe in the cities they used to know and love—"Hey! Where did everyone go? How can the Lower East Side look like *this* now?"—but it is also well-documented and statistically verified. And these processes are bending the arc of cities as an idea, of how we think cities can and should operate.

It is true that for the first time in world history more than half the world's population lives in cities. But look a little closer, and it's far more true to say the vast majority of people live in *sub*urban areas. In city after city across North America, suburbs, exurbs, periburbs, postsuburbs, concrete suburbs, and ethnoburbs are growing significantly faster than central cities, a familiar phenomenon that is mirrored across the globe in barrios, *banlieues*, "new towns," shantytowns, *gecekondus*, *favelas* and a thousand different variations.

As a 2014 *Economist* article put it, describing a phenomenon that has not abated: "In developed and developing worlds, outskirts are growing faster than cores. This is not the great urbanisation. It is the great suburbanisation."[4] It's not just residents that are being suburbanized; jobs are too. Starting in the mid-1990s, North America has seen the rapid decentralization of employment across essentially every sector. A 2009 Brookings Institution report analyzing the first phases of this pattern noted, "In almost every major industry, jobs shifted away from the city center between 1998 and 2006 . . . Employment steadily decentralized between 1998 and 2006: 95 out of 98 metro areas saw a decrease in the share of jobs located within three miles of downtown."[5] It is a trend that has continued apace into the 2020s and then accelerated again as cities and most every industry grapple with the repercussions of the pandemic. Working from home, job dislocation, desire for outside space, constant rent increases, downsizing, Covid claustrophobia, labor market transformations and good ole displacement have meant an intensification of sprawl and the movement out of inner cities.[6]

This radical reshaping of inner cities is closely entangled with the ongoing suburbanization of poverty across North America, mimicking what has long been unfolding in many parts of the globe. And, of course, the suburbanization of poverty closely tracks a commensurate process of the steady racialization of suburbs.[7] Researcher John Sullivan writes that, starting in the 2000s, "the proportion of the black population living in the biggest city of a given metropolitan area [in the United States] decreased in all 20 of the nation's largest metro areas."[8] People still tend to think about suburbs and the peripheral zones around major cities using specific and often calcified analytical lenses. Increasingly, those perceptions are being challenged in multiple ways, not the least of which is the economic contours of both inner and outer suburbs: "Today, more poor people live in the suburbs (16.4 million of them) than in U.S. cities (13.4 million), despite the perception that poverty remains a uniquely urban problem."[9] As the Brookings Institution put it in 2022, using data from the 2020 Census:

> All major racial groups are more likely to live in the suburbs than cities . . . Big suburbs' populations are more diverse that the total U.S. population . . . All of the past decades' growth in big suburbs is attributable to people of color . . .
>
> The growth of America's suburbs embodies the nation's population growth, accompanied by greater diversity due to the in-migration of new and long-standing minorities from nearby cities, from other parts of the country, and from abroad, as well as a rising multicultural youth population as families of color—like their earlier white counterparts—find the suburbs an ideal destination for raising children and forming new communities. From this perspective, the suburbs, perhaps more than anywhere else, are symbolic of America's rising diversity.[10]

Willow Lung-Aman echoed this in on NPR's *All Things Considered* in 2022: "I think it has been, really, a great migration in terms of the location of people of color and immigrants . . . You're seeing majority Black and brown suburbs that just a decade ago were majority white."[11]

There are scores of other examples that I might cite. As William H. Frey said in a November 2014 *New Republic* article, "The Suburbs: Not Just for White People Anymore": "For the first time, more of the minority population in the nation's largest metropolitan areas lives in the suburbs than in the city . . . Hispanics, Asians, blacks and other groups are becoming primary engines of growth in the nation's suburbs in an era when the aging white population will be barely holding its own."[12] Frey followed that comment up in 2022, analyzing US Census data and noting that in 2020 more than 60 percent of all Latino or Hispanic Americans and Asian Americans and 54 percent of Black residents lived in suburbs: "In 1990, roughly two out of 10 suburbanites were people of color. This rose to 30% in 2000 and 45% in 2020 [and] . . . people of color comprised more than half the suburban populations in 15 of the nation's 56 major metro areas."[13]

And it's not just North America. Consider Britain, for example. Geographers at Leeds University in the UK used census data to track internal migrations and found that "minorities were leaving core city neighbourhoods for lower-density suburban areas. In London, all minority groups are drifting out of the inner city. The trend in also noticeable around most other English cities, including Leeds, Birmingham, Nottingham and Leicester."[14] And, of course, poverty is also suburbanizing in the UK: "There are now more people living in poverty in outer London (1.22 million) than in the centre of the city (1.02 million)—something that wasn't the case 10 years ago, and which it says cannot be ignored in anti-poverty strategies."[15]

These patterns are evident in the most suburban of countries and are replicating the fractured natures of peripheralization that have existed for a very long time in cities across the Global South. The complex character of suburbia has always been evident to anyone who cares to look closely, and observers have been messing with tidy suburban clichés for generations. But today, new patterns of settlement—especially in the context of racial capitalisms, new orderings of poverty and urban displacements—are presenting a novel set of circumstances and disordering everything orthodox urbanism wants to claim about and for cities. We need to find some new languages, some new vocabularies for thinking about what is happening around us, because what we have on hand now is clearly insufficient.

3

Despite the extravagant evidence that we live on a *suburban* planet, most urban theory—and especially progressive urban theory—has been excessively slow to acknowledge and engage with new forms of urban peripheralization. That 100 percent includes me. My guess is that endemic scholarly dismissal of suburbanity owes substantially to our generalized urban snootiness: partly a disdain for lifestyles perceived as déclassé and unsophisticated, and partly an unwillingness to spend time in ostensibly distasteful areas far afield from the comfortable surroundings most researchers restrict themselves to.

This may be a little ungenerous. The suburbanization of poverty is happening in unfamiliar and asymmetric tempos, which makes it difficult to chart and creates a radically new set of circumstances for urbanists to confront. It's really hard—for a variety of interlocking reasons—to figure out how to approach suburbias, intellectually and socially as much as physically.

I am as surprised as anyone to find myself so interested in suburbs. I grew up in rural British Columbia, a fourth-generation settler on the West Coast: a white, Waspy punk rock kid transfixed by everything urban. All the music, all the books, all the movies, all the stories—everything that excited me was happening downtown in big cities. Like so many other kids from small towns and backwoods, I was desperate to escape and get to the busiest, most crowded cities possible—anywhere there was real action. And loving the city necessarily meant hating the suburbs—the bland, white, repressed, conformist, culturally eviscerated suburbs.

I didn't know anything about suburbs—any more than I knew anything about cities. I do not think I had ever really been in an actual suburb; I just knew I loathed them and everything they stood for. But, of course, I was predictably happy to hold aggressively defended and shouty opinions on subjects that I knew almost nothing about, opinions that easily bled into my adult life, peacefully unburdened by any real experience or knowledge.

I carry those presumptions with me still. I frequently find myself defaulting to ossified characterizations and stereotypes of suburbia that are not rooted in anything—neither data, experience, nor any good scholarship—I have encountered. And that's true for so much urban writing: people invoke the suburbs with tired tropes they deploy primarily to buttress easy and mostly apolitical narratives.

Take, for example, that old assumption that all suburbs are basically Wonder Bread reconstituted in residential form. Urban peripheries have almost always been viewed as black holes of white homogeneity while cities, especially inner cities, are awash in diversity. But the rapid racialization and suburbanization of poverty has begun to create a very different story: as so many inner cities are becoming richer and whiter, urban edges are emerging as more vibrant and racially diverse. Think about cities you know and love, think of the most diverse places there, and almost without exception you'll think of urban exclaves on the fringes of the inner metropole. But still, our discourse fails to reflect what everyone sees. As R. L'Heureux Lewis-McCoy put it to the *New York Times* in 2021: "We know that now, in the nation's largest metropolitan areas, the majority of Black residents live in the suburbs. Now the majority of immigrants live in the suburbs. Now the majority of Latinx and Asian Americans live there. But most news media, when they say 'suburban,' they mean 'white.'"[16]

Consider Ferguson, Missouri. I had never heard of the place before 2014, and when I read the first reports of murderous white police and Black riots, I just assumed it was a core city neighborhood in St. Louis. I had no idea it is a classic working-class suburb and that, like so many other suburbs, it had a much more complex demographic history than I imagined.

How about Levittown, New Jersey, one of *the* iconic North American suburbs? Founded in 1958 as the third Levittown ever built (the first two were in New York and Pennsylvania), it originally banned Black people from living there and was subsequently made famous by sociologist Herbert Gans's 1967 book *The Levittowners*, still one of urban sociology's best-known studies of local community life. As of 2020, it is 73 percent Black and only 17 percent white and is called Willingboro Township.[17] How about Maryvale, a metastasizing suburb of Phoenix? It was in the news in the 1980s when white people began abandoning ship after an unexplained outbreak of leukemia, and as of 2020 it is 76 percent Hispanic and less than 15 percent white.[18]

This trajectory holds true in Canada as well. Rising rents and home prices make it implausible for most non-wealthy newcomers to this country to consider settling in core city neighborhoods, and thus the major "ethnoburb" clusters around big Canadian cities are seeing an accelerating volume of new arrivals. As Statistics Canada puts it: "There is now a greater tendency among newcomers to settle in peripheral municipalities, most often those bordering a central municipality . . . Settling initially in a central municipality is no longer the predominant settlement pattern of immigrants to Canada."[19]

This will be obvious to anyone who spends time in any big Canadian city. A 2017 research paper from StatsCan underlined how Vancouver exhibits this pattern most distinctly, where "the suburbanization rate [of immigrants] increased from 66% in 2001 to 72% in 2011." In all three of Canada's major cities (Montreal, Toronto and Vancouver), earlier immigrant populations, from the British Isles, the United States, France and Germany, have dispersed across the metropolis, while "conversely, the groups with a more recent presence in Canada, for example, people from the Philippines, India, Bangladesh, Ghana and Iran, are also more concentrated in their settlement patterns." Those settlement concentrations are almost exclusively on the urban periphery.[20]

As Carlos Teixeira, a scholar of immigrant settlement and housing at University of British Columbia–Okanagan points out, up until the 1990s, migrants to Canada almost exclusively settled in Montreal, Toronto or Vancouver, but for the past thirty years, as census data continues to confirm, long-standing immigrant groups have begun to move out of the central cities to settle in suburbs.

But newer immigrant populations did not replace the older ones in urban cores—they headed directly to the suburbs as well. As Teixeira's explained to me:

> Established immigrants—some who owned property and real estate, others who were displaced by gentrification—started moving to the suburbs in search of better housing, backyards, better schools, and suddenly those suburbs started really growing. And then newer immigrants bypassed cities and went directly to the suburbs where they had families, friends, jobs, and there are communities they could connect with. Now some higher- and middle-income immigrants, as well as poorer migrants and refugees, are all the new reality of suburbs in Canada.[21]

Canadian cities are now often touted as among the most diverse in the world. Analysts, often using the language of multiculturalism, point to percentages of foreign-born residents, numbers of languages spoken, and/or mixes of various racialized ("visible minority") residents. In many of these categories, big Canadian cities tend to reside near the very top of global rankings.

But it really depends on what you think you are measuring and where you draw your boundaries: it is the larger metro areas that are increasingly home to newcomers, not the central cities. This is certainly true in Vancouver, which gets far more "diverse"— that is, far more Black and brown—as you exit the inner city. Eventually you come out the other side and leave the suburbs to find yourself in the rural, small-town far edges of the region that are overwhelmingly white, but you have to go pretty far to see the intensive "multiculturalism" peter out.[22] This pattern is never even or simple—there are all kinds of differentiated pockets and anomalies, instabilities and neighborhoods that don't fit the pattern, but the basic point is unmistakable: there is very little about modern suburbs that adhere to easy clichés.

This has been true outside North America for a very long time. Across the globe the same complex patterns of wealth and poverty and concentration and dispersal are equally evident in peripheralized communities on the urban fringes. Most cities were largely spared the great American (and Canadian, Australian, British and some northern European) highway and suburban build-out during the postwar boom, and thus peripheral urban areas have always been understood as complex and shifting. It was only that supernova explosion of cash across the Global Northern landscape that allowed for classic suburbia to be built in the first place, but it still exerts a powerful pull on our urban worldviews.

4

It is not just that suburbs are a lot more racially diverse than depictions in *Edward Scissorhands*, *Mad Men* or *The Stepford Wives* might have it, but there are now kaleidoscopic kinds of poverty and class striations marking the peripheries of every city. These are not just the forms of oft-claimed cultural or spiritual poverty or whatever that are supposed to be hallmarks of suburbia, but everyday, material deprivations and lacks. The suburbanization of poverty is real, as Elizabeth Kneebone details:

> The rapid pace of growth in the suburban poor population during the 2000s fueled a significant "tipping point" in the geography of the nation's poor. For the first time, American suburbs became home to more poor residents than cities. In 2015, 16 million poor people lived in the suburbs, outnumbering the poor population in cities by more than 3 million, small metro areas by more than 6 million, and rural areas by more than 8 million.[23]

There are some disputes over these numbers, with some observers noting that because the gross numbers of people living in suburbs are so much greater than in inner cities, of course there will be more poor people there. This is true, as Joe Cortright argues: "Poverty is highly unevenly distributed across metropolitan areas, and is far more concentrated in urban centers . . . Neighborhoods of concentrated poverty are still disproportionately found in cities."[24] But of course they are—cities by definition are denser. That said, there is no longer any question that it is increasingly untenable to cling to the easy trope of white middle- and upper-class suburbs concentrically surrounding poor, Black, immigrant inner cities.

The phenomenon of growing peripheralized poverty is even more verifiable on the ground and is closely related to the remaking of post-industrial urban cores. As contemporary cities are reimagined as newly capitalized investment opportunities, upscale residential reoccupations become the norm, demanding new social, cultural and built landscapes. The repercussions necessarily include continual waves of rearrangement, and many cities are actively interested in centrifugally displacing their less-productive residents and commercial enterprises. As Elizabeth Kneebone notes, in the United States these patterns are not new and have been underway for decades: "Almost every major metro area saw suburban poverty not only grow during the 2000s but also become more concentrated in high-poverty neighborhoods. By 2008–2012, 38 percent of poor residents in the suburbs lived in neighborhoods with poverty rates of 20 percent or higher. For poor black residents in those communities, the figure was 53 percent."[25]

Theorists have been anticipating and charting neoliberal urban restructuring since the 1970s. A number of simultaneous state economic interventions designed to incentivize, stimulate and support the liberties of intensive capital formation, combined with the forces of downsizing and offshoring, have put cities in remarkably fraught positions.

Staggering under the weight of historic levels of in-migration, starved for investment, and facing the loss of their manufacturing and industrial bases, cities are hungrily financializing and servicizing, restructuring spatially as much as economically. The resulting deep social polarizations induced commentators like Saskia Sassen and Manuel Castells to prophesize the emergence of "dual cities," or "hour-glass cities," with entrenching high-end wealth, atrophying middle classes and exploding lower classes remaking metropolitan geographies.

This strain of theory suggests that increasing social and income inequalities create mismatches between employment and housing—people find themselves living in the wrong places and too far from their work—and that cities thus have had to instigate new forms of corrective reordering. As cities performatively court international capital and professionals in highly capitalized and financialized industries, they therefore need to develop a stock of appropriate downtown residential and cultural attributes. Similarly, as lower-paid, industrial, service and manufacturing work is peripheralized, residential restructuring tends to follow. As industry vacates inner cities, those tracts of land (and very often the same buildings) are remade as condos, "authentic" shopping experiences and upscale cafés with very attractive brick walls and high ceilings. As bourgeois and wealthier residents abandon suburbia for "smart," walkable neighborhoods, less wealthy people who are escaping the exploding housing costs of the city are ready and willing to take their place.

This is a tidy and rather North American–centric story I am telling here, and it is tempting to think about all this as straightforward displacement/replacement. This narrative claims that the poverty once emblematic of (and virtually synonymous with) inner cities is being centrifugally removed and rearranged on the urban edges, while the suburban wealth that once concentrated on the outskirts of cities is now elbowing its way back in. Alan Ehrenhalt, among others, has floated a theory that casts these shifts as the "Great Inversion": "The late twentieth century was the age of poor inner cities and wealthy suburbs; the twenty-first century is emerging as an age of affluent inner neighborhoods and immigrants settling on the outside."[26] It would be convenient if that was the whole story, but it is significantly more complicated than that. The inversion thesis draws some rough outlines but needs a ton more analytical and political nuance.

I think these general theoretical threads about the neoliberal remaking of contemporary cities are largely correct. It is certainly true that many suburbs are marked by new poverty, often in severe pockets, but it is not just the result of new people moving in: it is often structural economic changes that are compromising the fortunes of existing residents.

It is also not true to say that all core city neighborhoods are now exclusively the province of elites. There are still entrenched concentrations of poverty in every inner city, and major swaths of suburbs that are still wealthy, exclusive and white. Urban restructuring is complicated, fractured and extremely volatile. There are wildly differential patterns emerging both internationally and intra-nationally, and even within individual cities, there are contradictory ebbs, flows, and side eddies, backwashes and riptides. It is increasingly clear, though, that new forms of social and spatial segregations are emerging across the globe, and that centrifugality, or peripheralization, is now almost always a critical feature of the process.

This thesis is of little surprise to many people living in cities outside North America. In so many places around the world, poor people and recent arrivals have been concentrated and segregated in banlieues and squatter towns and favelas and townships and *gecekondus* forever, long unwelcomed in central cities. *Sub*-urbs in many, maybe even most, parts of the world have almost nothing in common with the *suburbs* of the American imaginaries. It may well be, in fact, that what we in North America reflexively speak of as *suburbia* is a very temporally and spatially specific phenomenon, which we are now witnessing the dismantling of.

Contemporary American suburbs both created and were creations of that vast post–World War II American economic expansionism. In the throes of an emergent Cold War and faced with a mass return of soldiers, a spectacular baby boom and a nationwide housing shortage, the United States poured immense resources into tract housing construction, subsidized home-ownership and highway building. Prewar suburbs in America were "as socially diverse as the cities that they surrounded," observe Richard Harris and Robert Lewis. "Ironically, this heterogeneous landscape, and especially the open spaces lying between and beyond it, was the setting for a massive wave of postwar suburbanization that was characterized by similarity and standardization."[27]

This blast of money and resources inflated a fantastical suburban bubble, one unlike any other in scope or scale, which is apparently just now exhausting itself. Historically, suburbs have been a far more variegated, complicating and fractured landscape. The etymology of the word *suburb* speaks to the presumptions, common since antiquity, that undesirables—the very poor, sex workers, criminals, the mentally ill—who were deemed undeserving of the city's protection should be forced to stay in makeshift settlements outside the city walls, often crowded underneath them. In most parts of the world, and for most of urban history, *suburbs* have mostly meant *less than*, lower, below, secondary to the city, the *sub* to the *urb*.

But at the same time, as long as cities have been crowded, wealthier residents have sought escape in villas and dachas and estates and manors and palaces. Deliberately isolated and disconnected from urban tumult, these safe houses often gestured toward the modern North American version of a gated suburb: segregated, securitized and exclusive.

This multiple and shifting character of settlements outside the city walls was disrupted by that fifty-year suburban building frenzy in North America—often quasi-emulated elsewhere—to capitalize on the neoliberal convergence of a massive population expansion, spectacular proliferation of cheap credit, racialized paranoias driven by official and unofficial policy, and an aggressive governmental fetishization of homeownership. This particular suburban fantasy is now dissolving as suburbs everywhere that were once exclusive, white and wealthy are fracturing amid new forms of urban expulsions, banishments and (re)segregations.

This tumultuous reordering of city regions presses all of urban studies and urban thinking to become less provincial, to become more capacious and to look well outside traditional central-city confines. Looking at actually existing cities demands that urban and suburban studies reorient to think of *sub-urban* studies, in the context of massive new forms of displacement and marginalization.

5

I have three entwined goals here. The first is to join a growing number of theorists who are working to cast a different light on urban peripheries. I'd like to help to recast the sub-urbanizations of racialized, migrant, working-class and poor populations in a more fulsome and generous light.

Traditional urban theory cares little for suburbs, and even less for the new sub-urbs except as a distasteful foil, exoticized fantasia, or technical problem, which creates significant theoretical and political blind spots. I am entirely unclear if these new patterns of peripheralization are a transient set of phenomena, but my instincts suggest that what we are currently witnessing portends a long-term, fundamental reorganization of urban space triggered by the confluence of neoliberal remakings of city cores, transnational migrations and respondent racisms, global warming, economic restructuring and revanchist urbanism.

These new forms of the sub-urbanization of poverty throw up a profound set of challenges for residents, organizers, activists, urbanists, scholars and planners of all kinds—and all of us need to think hard on our work in light of these new currents. As suburban theorist Roger Keil once said to me, "The bourgeois Left really only feels comfortable in urban environments, and its political program revolves around a built landscape of coffee shops, public spaces, walkable streets and public transit. We don't really know how to live otherwise."[28] I think this comment is on point, and certainly speaks to me directly.

As I have become increasingly interested in sub-urbs everywhere, but most especially in Surrey, where I now spend all my days, I have found myself in so many surprising situations and places, totally out of my element, unclear how to act and unsure what I am looking for. Over the past several years, I have been grateful to have been invited into mosques, temples, churches and gurdwaras. I have had countless meetings in mall food courts. I have taken buses that I was convinced were never going to arrive. I have been lost more times than I like to admit. I have tried to walk to many places that were not even vaguely within walking distance. I have gaped at new planning initiatives and housing tracts that do not remotely fit my idea of the good life. I have lost my sense of humor in many traffic jams.

But what I have found and keep finding here, and in every city I visit, are new (or at least new to me) and creative forms of social organization that are emerging on urban peripheries. New patterns of solidarities, new ways to confront social marginalization, new kinds of gathering spaces, and new ways of living are thriving within suburban landscapes, many of which do not adhere to my easy leftist imaginations.

Over the past few years, I have been in evangelical churches above auto body shops, pizza shops in garages and boutiques in industrial parks. I have done my share of afterhours drinking in plaza parking lots, shopped at fresh fruit and vegetable stands in mall food courts, played mini-golf in decommissioned suburban school gymnasiums, had a better-than-expected time at parties in sprawling chain restaurants, and attended protests and demonstrations taking over mall concourses. All these experiences have defied my easy stereotypes, helped me notice some of what I do not see, and leave me grasping for new theoretical languages and grammars.

For at least a couple of decades now, a small number of scholars have been using the term *post-suburbia* in a nod to the fractured, confused, confusing and recursively shifting patterns of contemporary peripheries.[29] *Post-suburbia* does not necessarily signify a binary departure/evolution from suburbia, but instead might be described as something that is emerging, as classical suburbia is "partly converted, inverted or subverted into a process that involves densification, complexification and diversification of the suburbanization process . . . Post-suburbanization also entails a profound re-scaling of the relations and modes of governance that have traditionally regulated the relationships between centre and periphery in the suburban model."[30] I'm frankly a little ambivalent about the term—as much as I am about its close cousins *edge cities, technoburbs, in-between cities,* or *fringe cities*—but all this points toward the right general assessment: that contemporary sub-urbanization doesn't look all that suburban anymore.

I am not—and do not want to become—any kind of apologist for extant suburbia. (And certainly have no interest in the Wendell Cox–Randal O'Toole schools of pro-sprawl, retrograde libertarian "urbanism.") Many, perhaps most, of the well-trod critiques stand: the grim isolations of the suburban built environment, the deep fetishization of the automobile, the fragmentation, the consumptiveness, the waste, the ecological perils—all of it pisses me off as much as anyone. I am not asking that anyone appreciate any particular existing suburban form. But I do want to challenge the condescending ease with which so much of progressive and leftist thought writes off massive parts of metropolitan regions where most of the urban population lives. Far too much of existing radical urban theory acknowledges gentrifications, but cares little where displaced people end up. And frankly speaking, I am absolutely guilty of this too.

Historically, the city has been conflated with modernity and democracy: the public milieus, the strangers, the difference, the shared institutions, the walkable scales—all of it supposedly nurtures Athenian ideals of the polis. I think that prescription is correct in some ways, but does that then mean that people who live in sub-urban regions are relegated to a less-robust modernity, are in a democratic deficit, are less capable of civic life? This is exactly the kind of inference that leads to so many suburbanites feeling condescended to. And then when suburbanites embrace weird parochial chauvinisms, urban analysts diagnose newcomers and working-class voters as suffering from some kind of false consciousness or misplaced priorities or ineffable malaise.

This is the legacy of the school of urbanism à la Jane Jacobs, Andrés Duany, Richard Florida: an aggressively aestheticized neoliberal vision of the city that prioritizes a very particular kind of "vibrancy" as the scenery for bourgeois fantasies of public life. The New Urbanist worldview cares little for class or race, lionizing sanitized landscapes of "alive" shopping districts, public spaces and mixed uses.

Much of Jacobs's work—and the New Urbanists and her apologists since—reads like a gentrification how-to manual, a willful disregard for politics of property that leaves a path littered with one decimated, sanitized neighborhood after another. It has laid the intellectual foundations for the reoccupations of inner cities by those who are seeking an "authentic" urban experience and have the money to buy it. Progressive urbanist fascination with Paris seems to come just short of overtly pining for a revived pan-Hausmannization that can sweep clear the poor with mass evictions and remake any city with a cleaner, more-ordered, nostalgically bourgeois facade. For the New Urbanists, the sub-urbs are just an icky laughingstock, a sneering punchline to jokes told with little curiosity about the social forces that create them, nor generosity about the social milieus that flourish there.

The only substantive engagement most progressive urbanists today have with sub-urbs is to offer boilerplate templates for walkable high streets, densification, transit-oriented planning, compact communities and bike lanes. I find it particularly galling to hear the confident prescriptions for "fixing" the suburbs coming from the exact same mouths that have eviscerated inner-city neighborhoods and now want to foist the same "solutions" onto the only affordable areas left in the region.

Out here, smug calls for a "Vancouverist" remaking of Surrey are echoed by exactly the same people who have fucked over Vancouver, creating a place that year after year resides in the top tier of least affordable cities in the world. I see the same processes in so many cities—like in, say, Seattle, where poor neighborhoods throughout the southern part of the city are fighting proposed light rail extensions, with each new station creating another localized wave of displacement and reduction in bus services. Typically, communities will always welcome new and improved public transit—who doesn't want a train station nearby?—but when it instigates yet another Trojan horse wave of evictions, all this so-called smart-city, transit-oriented development is actually just another menace to everyday people. I see the same kinds of dynamics in every city I visit, the same blithely ignorant pseudo-progressivism trashing poor and working-class communities with a shrug. There is so much that needs changing in Surrey, just as in every sub-urb, but we cannot defer to the same tired formulas that are disfiguring inner cities across the globe.

These prescriptions for "fixing the suburbs" are further hamstrung by the misplaced confidence that easy divisions between the city and suburb can be drawn. Certain place names, along with all kinds of racialized clichés, are code for certain built forms. Here in Metro Vancouver, "Surrey" means endless cheap residential housing tracts and trashy malls, while "Vancouver" means glassy condo towers and bike lanes. But there are "town centers" in Surrey that are denser than most of Vancouver, and new towers are springing up by suburban SkyTrain transit hubs. Downtown Vancouver is very dense, but the vast bulk of the city is actually made up of single-family housing on large lots where everyone drives. The clean distinctions between sprawling burbs and dense cities rarely hold easily, and the edges where the city ends and the burbs begin are unclear, permeable and unfixed.

This is true in every city, and territorial borders are far more performative than material.

Consider density, for example. Most of us are pretty sure we know what it looks and feels like, but if you wanted to, and depending on where you draw the lines of demarcation, it is pretty easy to make an argument that the least sprawling city in America is not New York, as everyone assumes, but Los Angeles.[31] I've spent enough time in both places for such a distinction to confuse the hell out of me, but it just requires a creative touch and underlines the problem with trying to claim easy binary distinctions and drawing fixed borders. In every urban area, cities and suburbs are bound together, reflecting and constructing one another, and it is hard to say where one ends and the other starts. Imagining that it is somehow possible to talk about Surrey as separate from Vancouver, or Orange County as distinct from Los

Angeles, is to ignore the actually existing economic and social patterns of centering and peripheralizing.

Understanding what kinds of development are being allowed, what kinds of wealth and poverty are being created and where urban power resides necessarily means seeing cities and suburbs in relational contexts. Consider banlieues in France, for example, or favelas in Brazil, "new towns" in India, "lost cities" in Mexico, *gecekondus* in Turkey, commuter towns in China, shantytowns in Pakistan, slums in Nigeria, and all the wildly divergent patterns of peripheralization across the planet.

Each of these examples requires an examination of specific logics of social and spatial segregation that are generating new forms of accumulation alongside new forms of poverty. But we can pull on some common threads here. The globalized phenomenon of urban expulsions and banishments is not universalizable; it is articulated very differently in every city, though the processes that are driving these new spatial logics can be generally theorized. I am not interested in mapping or taxonomizing what are often assumed to be wild, uncharted urban peripheries but in understanding how sub-urban places fall off official maps and are rendered *outside*.

This is my first goal here: I want to push urban theory toward a more creatively engaged and generous approach to sub-urbs of all kinds. I am most curious here about the forms of displacement and dispossession that are buffeting sub-urbs from multiple directions. My first instinct is that this project necessarily means thinking through racialized capitalisms, and specifically, currently operating conceptions of property.

But that's not all of it: there are other stories at play here. My second goal in this book is to trouble the ontological underpinnings of center–periphery narratives, and to try and reimagine what we talk about when we talk about "the city."

One of my core problems in developing the analysis here is that the vocabularies I seem to have at hand are inadequate—actually, they are worse than that; they are distorting and regulating. I am really struggling for a grammar. So far in this book I have been using words like *suburbs*, *peripheries*, *edges*, *fringes*, *margins* —pinballing between terms without much clarity. In part that's because I am wholly dissatisfied with all of these. This is language that implicitly relegates certain parts of the urban to the "outside" and designates other parts—with pretty flimsy rationale—as the "center."

The languages of suburbs, peripheries and margins echo the logics of empires—placing colonial metropoles at the center of the world, with everything beyond existing merely as undeveloped, backward, dependent and subservient provinces. Those are not descriptive efforts; those languages actively constitute the places they designate, and our urban vocabularies are performing the same kinds of functions. For most urbanists and urban theorists, the suburbs are highly Orientalized—ugly, dark, mysterious, exoticized places where poor people now go to disappear into inscrutably car-infested placelessness.

You may have noted that a few pages back I started to use *sub-urbia* instead of *suburbia*. I am trying to recast/reframe peripheral urban communities outside the confines of conventional suburban discourses. I am using the hyphenated *sub-urb* to refer to a constellation of settlements outside city-wall borders that are positioned (both within and from afar) to be distastefully "less than," the *sub*, the *urb* in both class and race. *Sub-urbs*, as opposed to the *suburbs*, are a set of modes of living and ways of being that include the built form, but much more as well.

I am going to toggle between these terms on occasion, as the terms overlap and entwine. Most settlements on peripheries around the world, and increasingly most North American (and North American–style) suburbs are included in sub-urbia. I am not much interested in suburbs: they have been dissected and theorized sufficiently. But I am highly interested in sub-urbia. One of the core threads of this book is a struggle for terminology, not in a taxonomic sense, but in a search for useful ways to speak of new forms of banishments, relegations and displacements. How we speak of these reorderings is not just a descriptive exercise; it is always prescriptive. As a minor intervention, distinguishing and thinking through sub-urbia might be useful.

The "categories, codes and conventions" of most urban studies are actively sub-urbanizing and peripheralizing as we go, and dominant theory actively centers its presumptive "center," without much question. The languages (certainly including most of what I have been able to deploy thus far) are very explicitly performing marginalization as they purport to describe it. As Ananya Roy asks: "For whom is the city a coherent concept? Whose urban experience is stable and coherent? Who is able to see the city as a unified whole? By contrast, for whom is the city a geography of shards and fragments?"[32] The question of where a city starts and stops, and in whose interests it is so pressing to demarcate clear boundaries (and what lies outside them; who is expelled), leaps out here—even as I grasp for terms that do not reinscribe those same kinds of languages that cannot think past center/hinterlands, metropoles/colonies, empires/provinces, cities/peripheries.

It strikes me that there is never a "periphery": that is just an idea that is leveraged in the interests of power. The idea of what is "outside" describes that which does not count as part of the "center" and thus what does not really matter. The periphery is an idea that is actively constituted as a function of legitimizing accumulation and control. And this mode of thinking continues with the willing compliance of urbanists: the notion of the urban periphery performs a critical centering function. Why are the glassy condo towers, the exercises of high-end recreational shopping and the architectures of financialization that mark downtown Vancouver the "center" of this city? What are they the center *of* exactly, and whose politics are driving those definitions? In whose interests is it to insist on these kinds of taxonomies?

The notion of the "outside," of the "periphery," has very real and very material consequences. Some years ago, I was giving a talk in Surrey to an audience of planners, city officials, social service organizations and businesspeople. The event was one of those civic "visioning" exercises, a daylong series of events claiming to re/generate Surrey. The stated intent was to develop some new social and cultural energy as Surrey struggles to emerge as a full-fledged *city*. I offered some ideas around civic participation, grassroots organizing, and planning from below. It was essentially an anti-creative-class kind of talk.

After the lecture, a woman waited to speak with me. She was a city councilor and had ambitious ideas about her own future, and the question she asked hit me. "Okay, everything you said is fine and good, I agree with some of it," she said. "But here's the real problem: every young person with energy, ambition, or creativity desperately wants to leave Surrey. Most young people don't want to be here. They want to be in Vancouver, or Toronto, or Dubai, or Karachi, or anywhere not stuck in the suburbs. What can we do about this?"

I have thought about her question often. This is the same question that grips small towns, rural areas and agricultural communities across the planet. But the loss of ambitious young people is not the whole story. It is no doubt true that lots of young people want to leave for grander, sexier fields, but it really depends on who you are, the kinds of kids you know, and what kinds of questions you are posing. Some of the youth I know want to leave Surrey, sure, but honesty, hardly any of them talk about that as a driving goal. I know a whole lot of young people, and most are energetically proud of Surrey, will defend it to anyone and imagine long horizons here.

My day-to-day work is co-directing a project called Solid State Community Industries, which I co-founded. We are building a solidarity economy in Surrey with racialized migrant communities, which is both the product and source of most of my ongoing interest and research in suburbs. Surrey is an hour via public transit from downtown Vancouver, and while everyone gets into the city sometimes, to shop or go to dinner or a show or whatever, few people I know seem particularly drawn to the "central" city. For almost all my friends and colleagues, their centers of social gravity are their families, universities, schools, mosques, gurdwaras, churches or parks, all of which are in Surrey or an adjacent suburb. They go to school locally, hang out in Surrey malls, play sports, participate in clubs and go to their place of worship, but it is manifestly clear that very few people I know actively "center" downtown Vancouver. And honestly, neither do I anymore.

I still go into inner-city Vancouver now and then, but now that I spend all my days in Surrey and we've moved onto a houseboat in the next suburb over, my whole point of view and reference points have shifted. I almost never feel any FOMO, nor do I feel like I have been expelled or am somehow on the outside. It's been a huge and unexpected shift: a few years ago, if I spent any time in the suburbs, I would have felt like I was just out of it, but now all my centers have moved, and it feels to me like downtown is missing all the action. It makes me think about how imagined urban cartographies constantly orient and reorient political fidelities.

This of course closely echoes postcolonial city theory, which is a potent vehicle for conceptualizing the urban—and suburban—and offers sweet respite from the relentless insistences of most contemporary global city posturing. In the wake of dramatic urban restructuring triggered by neoliberalism and globalizing economies, global city theory emerged in the 1990s as perhaps the dominant analytical vehicle for contemporary urban research. With research roots as far back as the 1960s, global city theory has described emerging global geographies where flows of capital, information, goods and people carve new circuits that pay little heed to Westphalian lines of demarcation. Instead, it sees a world that can be classed and ranked in urban hierarchies, with massive concentrations of financial and modern mercantilist power accumulating in alpha cities. These hubs are the command-and-control centers of new networks and flows, possessing gravitational fields that agglomerate capital and highly financialized services, fracturing traditional relationships between cities and their local regions.

The influence of global city theory can scarcely be underestimated and continues to offer profound insights, remake research agendas and transform civic priorities. It also performs a very powerful ordering function. Global city theory concretizes and deepens a fixation with a very select group of dominant cities by fetishizing financialization and capitalization, and then explicitly measuring cities against one another via sophisticated ranking systems. In the words of Jennifer Robinson, this relegates most cities, especially in the Global South, as "off the map." Robinson, and many of her postcolonial peers, call for research into the "ordinary cities" that are ignored and subjugated by dominant theory.[33]

In precisely the same kinds of ways that urban theory in general, and global city theory specifically, lionizes certain cities and consigns "lesser" cities to the peripheries of legitimate inquiry, dominant urban theory marginalizes anywhere outside imagined city boundaries as the *sub* to the *urb*. These are not apolitical research cartographies; they are exercises of power, taking care to highlight some elements and leave others out, constructing and ordering what counts.

But global city theory is not just making shit up. There absolutely *are* critical restructurings underway in (and between) cities across the globe—shifts and movements that are distancing more and more people from loci of power, decision-making, control and capital. The spatial and structural forms of these new peripheralizations give permission to one another and continue to aggregate capital and power in a small number of cities and an ever-smaller number of hands. Global city theorists, though, have to answer the same questions as any researcher: In whose interest is this work being deployed? Who is included, who is excluded, who is participating in what, who is telling whose stories, and what kinds of ordering is the research performing?

Which gets us back to the sub-urbs. It is clear that in cities across the globe, *something* is happening, something perhaps unprecedented. But how to speak of it? Is it one major process, a collection of processes, particular things in particular places? Is there a thread to pull that can offer insight into various kinds of peripheries? I'm curious about new vocabularies that can describe actually existing places but can also be applicable generally. I'm not sure if the particularities of Surrey have anything to say to peripheral zones anywhere else—to barrios, tent cities, slums, shantytowns, *borgatas*, favelas, *chabolas*, squatter villages, banlieues or sub-urbs—but my guess is that there are some common structural processes and common narratives at play, at least in part or in fractured, reassembled forms.

Centers and peripheries are not static ideas and there is never any one center. In any city, there are endless centers, big and small, centering various kinds of activities, forming and reforming, making and remaking. Some of those centers are in fact downtown—pivots of tourism and investment, finance and real estate speculation—but there are many others, visible and obscured, and many of those exist on what are ostensibly "peripheries."

I think what I am most interested in is the *process* of centering, and by consequence, of peripheralizing. Contemporary urban restructuring is characterized by massive exclusions, displacements and dispossessions, and I think the right questions to ask are: Who is getting excluded from what, by whom and on what auspices? Who decides who is *inside* and who is *outside*—and inside or outside *what*? And what are the centrifugal forces that are ejecting low-income and racialized residents out from particular kinds of centers?

But here again, the vocabulary gets tricky. I just used the words *exclusions* and *ejecting*, but are they the right ones? There is an expansive set of explanatory frameworks employed to describe how people are shifting and being shifted around in contemporary cities. Various theorists argue for terms such as *expropriation, expulsion, dispossession, displacement, gentrification, banishment, evictions, exploitation, peripheralization, suburbanization* and/or *marginalization* (there are others!), and each of these has specific value and unclarities. It really helps to have descriptive languages when we are trying to make sense of what's going on around us, especially when we are trying to figure out how to resist. This may seem overly punctilious: we can see urban crises of displacement all around us, but how does this analytical contortionism help?

Maybe most critically, we have to figure out how to fight the disfigurements so many cities we love are suffering. We all want to start throwing some punches, but where to aim? Swinging wildly is just as likely to clip a friend as it is a foe. But there's more, too. How we speak of these processes and functions has repercussions and can groove lines of analysis that are often tricky ruts to escape. Take *dispossession*, for example, which is a word I have been interested in for a long time. It is an evocative and powerful concept, but in the context of land battles, it is fraught. *Dispossession* implies an originary "possession" that has been violated. *Dispossession* fixes certain kinds of property relations—the exact kinds of conceptions of property that many leftist claims (and many theorists from disparate traditions) are trying to unsettle—and slyly insists on property models of ownership and exclusive sovereignty. If we fight back against dispossession, is the implied answer a deepened commitment to possession?[34]

There is never one master process at play anywhere. There are always multiple unstable, competing and complementing forces at work in any place, but we can look closely, ask after specific experiences and specific examples, and theorize their origins and repercussions. I am happy to work both inductively and deductively here and want to propose some new analytical frames for thinking about sub-urbanisms.

In thinking about generating new urban grammars, I want to pay particular attention to the (often very subtle) dismissive, degrading or marginalizing implications of new conceptual apparatuses—and especially how they land for residents who live far from certain loci of power. In the same ways that the brilliant critiques of global city theory unsettle its implicit ordering work, it is useful to keep noticing how certain terms—like *suburban*, for example—and certain kinds of analysis perform the same kinds of functions.

Let me give you a very particular example. Like so many people, I have been grappling with how to think about displacement and gentrification for a long time. In 2016 I published a book called *What a City Is For*.[35] That book focuses on a single neighborhood in Portland, Oregon—Albina—that was at one time the city's only majority-Black district. In the wake of an aggressive urban renewal program from 1990 to 2010, Albina saw upward of ten thousand Black people displaced and replaced by white residents. It's a tragedy: Portland has broken something that cannot be fixed, and a whole community has been dispersed. The displaced residents did not move to any one single area; they settled in a whole variety of new neighborhoods, mostly much further afield, where Portland's famous urban design features are in slim supply.

In my research for the book, I spent a lot of time in Albina over a number of years, walked every nook and cranny of the neighborhood, made many friends, interviewed all kinds of local activists, politicians, researchers and residents. Immodestly, I still think it's a good book, one that tries to ask some fundamental questions about contemporary displacements, and thinks through property, sovereignty and all the entwined racial logics. I really tried hard to understand what had happened to Albina.

But what is curious to me in retrospect is that I paid so much attention to the neighborhood that had been gentrified, and so little on the people who had been displaced. That book fixated on the physical place that once was a vibrant Black neighborhood and did not think to follow the people who left. Where did they go? What happened to them? Are they just lost in some suburban wilderness? I really doubt it—I'm guessing most of those people have built new lives, new patterns, new kinds of solidarities in new places. People there suffered through a shitty circumstance and some terrible civic policy, but they are not passive victims. Somehow, in telling the story of Albina, I ghosted some of the most critical actors out of the story.

I'm not fundamentally down on that book, but it highlights a series of questions for me, and I still wonder how I failed to ask after those people. It wasn't through ill will, or lack of research, or a lack of time. The book had a blind spot, or maybe a couple of overlapping blind spots, and deferred to extant narratives of gentrification. I want to pay close attention to the ease with which certain people get written out of stories, and how certain modes of thinking make that so easy. I am going to test out some new vocabularies throughout this book. I do not yet have convenient replacements on hand for the grammar of *suburb*, *periphery*, *margins*, and so on, but I do think that through some theorizing and research I might be able to get there.

That's my second goal here. I want to join those who are challenging center and periphery conceptions and seeking new ways to talk about sub/urban displacements, expulsions and dispossessions.

7

My third goal in this book is somewhat more pointed. There is something of a lacuna currently in radical urban theory. Perhaps daunted by the sheer pace and power of neoliberal restructuring, too many critical urban scholars have retreated too far into the academy, rarely poking their heads out, and the result is a current moment in the theoretical trajectory that is needlessly timid. This is true at least for most institutionalized discourses: on the ground, there is a startling rise in sophisticated urban activist theory, impelled and inspired by a bushel of new and revived movements. Driven by people's sense of exhaustion with national-level electoral landscapes and the immediacy of urban battles, the most transformative political organizing, everywhere you look across the globe, is happening at the city scale. Municipalist movements, fearless city networks, sanctuary and refuge cities, food justice work, anti-fascist and anti-racist activism, libertarian municipalism, Black Lives Matter, Idle No More, Right to the City alliances, anti-austerity riots, squatting and tenant organizing, urban solidarity economies, migrant justice . . . there's so much more, but you get my point. Among my claims here is that every one of these movements in the *urb* has to learn to speak directly to the *sub*, and that if you look a little closer, many of those movement's most powerful energies are emanating from well outside inner cities.

Equally, I want to challenge suburban research to do much more. Contemporary suburban theory, both scholarly and activist, is ripe for a more fulsome and generative radical analysis. Frankly speaking, I want suburban theory to brazenly contribute to revolt and refusal. I don't want to call for "politicizing or democratizing the suburbs," or "dissent," or "critique," or an "engaged research agenda" or any other tepid contemporary academic BS. I think we should be unapologetically organizing for revolt and refusals in the plainest sense. I want scholarship and research to actively contribute to a radically transformed set of social relations in the *sub* as much as the *urb*.

We live in an era where commentators can scarcely find the words to describe the incredible concentrations of wealth that are accumulating in ever-fewer hands. As soon as one report emerges documenting exactly how much the 1 percent or the 0.1 percent controls relative to the bottom four billion, or the bottom two-thirds or whatever, another even-more-ghastly set of figures trumps the previous one.

We are also living through a time of unprecedentedly grave ecological perils. Global warming is only one among many threats to extant forms of life on earth. The domination of humans by other humans gives permission to humankind's domination of the natural world and vice versa: they are expressions of the same extractive and exploitative worldview. Confronting each of today's explosive inequality and ecological crises requires a set of fundamental political re-orientations—which has to begin with a renovated politics of land.

And what are urban peripheries other than capitalism's need to move its problems around? Sub-urbs—in all their variation—are really just different iterations of spatial segregations trying to ameliorate urban crises. Capitalism only functions if one or more parts of the Land–Labor–Capital triad is stolen via colonialism, land theft, slavery, surplus labor, and so on. The only other temporary alternative is to defer the actual costs through financial debt, ecological debt, collective debt, and personal debt. Capital's spatial fix is part of this process—pushing problems around, forestalling disaster, shifting crises.

Jamie Peck has advanced the thesis that suburbs are neoliberal frontiers—places where capital escaped to during a historical regulatory movement in cities. In a 2011 paper, he argues:

Since the 1970s, suburbia has become a significant, but perhaps underappreciated, spatial expression of neoliberalism's deregulatory moment ... Suburbia has become a strategically significant nexus for open-ended, deregulatory experimentation, systematically favoring more decentralized, privatist, and market-oriented approaches ... So positioned, as a kind of deregulatory ebb tide against centralized, municipal (over)regulation, metropolitan planning, and sociospatial redistribution, the suburbs have exerted an increasingly strong (but often almost silent) undertow on political life and regulatory capacities in the United States.[36]

I think this is a useful, if insufficient, theoretical line to pursue. The analysis here is way too reductionist and too predictably full of Anglo-American cliché that reverts to the same simple stereotypes about suburbs, rather than actually looking at suburbs as they actually exist. But I think about Peck's paper all the time. It is clear that Surrey is—in part—being shaped by capital escaping the perceived burdens of building, zoning and environmental rules and regulations in Vancouver, running to the suburbs for freer pastures to roam. Former students of mine who have found planning work in Surrey's municipal offices speak of developers brazenly refusing to comply with any enforcement of city regulations, instead going above the offices' heads with clocklike regularity to get exemptions. Look from one direction and it sure seems like "open-ended, deregulatory experimentation, systematically favoring more decentralized, privatist, and market-oriented approaches" is in full flower in Surrey.

But also, not so much.

Like all binaries, the "highly regulatory city vs. the Wild West burbs" distinction only sort of works if you squint at the evidence in just the right way. Under any sustained scrutiny, the easy dualisms start dissolving. The idea that Vancouver, for example, is some kind of regulatory sinkhole where capital is endlessly mired in statist bureaucracy may well be true for some but is spectacularly untrue for most: Vancouver represents one of the most fulsome expressions of neoliberal urbanism anywhere on the planet, and free-flowing property speculation is dominating the city landscape.

You could try to build another version of the "Great Inversion" argument and claim that, while North American cities once exhibited a Keynesian mode of development, they are now exuberantly welcoming capital back and the urban regulatory impulse is in full retreat. This argument may suggest that where postwar suburbs were once the pressure valve for capital accumulation, they are no longer needed in the same way now that capital is flowing back into urban cores.

Working in the wake of Marxist theorists like Richard Walker who view suburban growth as a kind of "capital switching," a solution to urban crises of overproduction and stagnation, Peck gestures to the "the zigzagging course of neoliberalization."[37] I think that gets closer to reality, and Peck is on surer ground when he theorizes sub-urbs as "subversive" of the *urb*. He means that in the sense of undermining regulatory agendas, but I'd like to submit that if the sub-urban landscape is understood more complexly, with a greater degree of nuance and generosity, than that "subversiveness" harbinges new kinds of hopefulness.

More often than not, I am coming to understand the sub-urbs in terms of alienation—in the classical Marxist sense for sure, but other ways as well. Cities have always aggregated and focused regional wealth, but today new forms of globalized capital accumulate spectacular levels of financialized and speculative wealth and power in urban centers. The pivot for contemporary concentrations of wealth is always racialized property, and as the contemporary fetishization of real estate leaks out of the city core, it inevitably inflects and infects both inner and outer suburbs in myriad ways.

Sub-urbs are defined by the reallocation and restructuring of time and space. I submit here that focusing on peripheralizations in the contexts of alienations, displacements and expulsions may offer some new routes to sub-urban subversions and revolts. Thinking about alienation has to mean being unafraid to ask after *fidelity*. That's not a word, or an idea, that many folks want to hang their hats on, but I think it is the right one here.

8

To live today is to be enveloped by precarities: by the anxieties of climate change, of turbulent economic and cultural reordering, of technological speed. The velocity of everyday change demands that we stay agile and flexible, ready to move, ready to adjust. The sheer pace of neoliberal restructuring keeps all of us on our toes, where sureties are way less sure tomorrow.

The idea of staying in one job, one house, one place for a generation (or many generations) sounds quaint. It sounds like a pastoralist ideal writ urban, but it is also the foundation for so much ecological thinking. The idea that people who are rooted in place, who belong to a place—and it to them—are necessarily more ecologically sensitive reverberates through environmentalist rhetorics and is an idea I regrettably have trafficked in myself. For a long time, I easily deferred to the cliché that people who have lived in one place over a duration will necessarily care more for that place, and thus will have an elevated ecological relationship with its more-than-human inhabitants.

Aside from the blatant lack of empirical evidence to support this claim, the idea that some people can and should belong to certain places bleeds easily into ethno-nationalisms, xenophobias and outright fascisms. The historical racism of so many environmental organizations is echoed by the ecological claims of so many far-right political parties across the globe. Anti-immigrant, pro-border violence is often animated by blood-and-soil claims to belonging: that certain people, and only those people, are able to care for "their" land.

Listen to Marine Le Pen from France's National Rally (formerly the National Front): "Environmentalism [is] the natural child of patriotism, because it's the natural child of rootedness

. . . If you're a nomad, you're not an environmentalist. Those who are nomadic . . . do not care about the environment; they have no homeland."[38] Or Tucker Carlson, the odious, race-baiting former Fox News commentator:

> Take a trip to our southwestern deserts, if you don't believe it. Thanks to illegal immigration, huge swaths of the region are covered with garbage and waste that degrade the soil and kill wildlife . . . Illegal immigration comes at a huge cost to our environment . . . The left used to care about the environment—the land, the water, the animals. They understood that America is beautiful because it is open and uncrowded. Not so long ago, environmentalists opposed mass immigration. They knew what the costs were. They still know. But they don't care.[39]

The suggestion that movement and migration make people less environmentally sensitive, less caring for the land, or less ecological is just rude, and bound up with settler-colonialist fixities and ethnonationalist violence. Every modern city is a neocolonial project, and every part of Metro Vancouver is built on stolen Indigenous land. The settler city and the settler suburb alike fetishize the "settled," of staying in one place over a duration, establishing a "here" and an "ours," a mode of possession that is eager to expel those who are not "us." Community and localist dogmas fetishize a mystical connection between people and place, easily turning it on anyone who is not "from here."

In his book *The Art of Not Being Governed*, James Scott details the topographies of Zomia, an area of something like two-and-half million square kilometers sprawling across the Southeast Asian Massif, encompassing parts of Vietnam, Laos, Thailand, Burma, China, Tibet, India and Pakistan. There are more than a hundred million people living in stateless configurations across Zomia, populated by refugees from the region's various states, fugitives who over the past two thousand years have fled conscription, taxation, corvee labour and capture at the hand of their governments, rejecting sedentary settlements and wet-rice-fueled agriculture, moving upward, out of the valleys into the mountains, essentially living above an elevation of three hundred meters.

Zomia contains thousands of shifting tribes and language groups, forming and reforming, often blending into one another, and reconstituting themselves, bound together by a non-fixity: "In the space of a hundred kilometers in the hills," Scott writes, "one can find more cultural variation—in language, dress, settlement pattern, ethnic identification, economic activity, and religious practices—than one would ever find in the lowland river valleys." Every aspect of Zomian life is built around movement; swidden (shifting, typically slash-and-burn) agriculture that can be left and returned to later, even if an invader burns the fields to the ground; villages that can be easily moved; malleable governance structures; and multilingualisms: "Virtually everything about these people's livelihoods, social organization, ideologies, and (more controversially) even their largely oral cultures, can be read as strategic positionings designed to keep the state at arm's length." Scott describes the statist project as attempting to weld disparate peoples together into fixed national identities built around sedentary agriculture, and the Zomian project as creating illegibilities to state control.[40]

I've long wondered if the Zomian example could translate to the urban. It feels akin: people fleeing the city, finding ways to resist through movement, refusing to be captured by untenable rents and property regimes, making themselves illegible to markets. It feels to me like so many people in Surrey and the suburbs surrounding Vancouver (my own family included) have done exactly that, and for many, there has been a double, or triple, movement—leaving unlivable circumstances in other parts of the world, crossing borders, mobility as an ongoing form of refusal.

Celebrating movement and borderlessness as a potent form of political refusal is not to fetishize nomadism, smooth space or whatever, but to *celebrate* non-fixity and refusals of all kinds. I do not think this celebration has to give up on the idea of rootedness. I am not interested in giving up the good fight, of turning tail when our neighborhoods or communities are threatened. We have to be able to stand and fight for places that we care about; we have to be able to dig in, plant roots, care for a place over a duration, and, sometimes, to not do so. We can celebrate both rootedness and mobilities in the same breath and politicize both equally.

The claims of Indigenous communities across the globe are rooted in their relationships to and with the land since time immemorial. Anti-colonial resistance rests on people resisting occupation and domination, refusing to step aside, refusing to move, refusing to give up their land. At the same time, refugees and migrants who have left are not giving up, nor are they rescinding their claims, nor are they less committed to resistance. Sovereignties are fluid, and borderlessness does not give permission to settler occupations, dispossessions and expulsions, nor does anyone's movement necessarily discredit their connection or claims to any lands.

Similarly, I think we have to turn urban resistance inside out, to construct an alternative arc of urban theory that doesn't victimize us, doesn't make us feel helpless. If rapacious markets are vampirically sucking the life out of neighborhoods, why not move, why not escape the stifling confines of absurd central cities? Why not reshape that movement, not as loss and lament, but as recentering our lives and refusing capture? Why not turn this story inside out?

What exactly are our fidelities to? If we fetishize an aesthetic rendition of what a city is supposed to look like, if we fixate on certain kinds of fixed centers, we blind ourselves to a whole world of possibilities.

9

When I thought about formalizing this research a little, the first place I thought of testing some of my ideas out was Portland, Oregon. It is close, just a jaunt down the West Coast, and it's a place I know well. Portland looks and feels a whole lot like Vancouver with its aggressively liberal whiteness, its bike lanes and craft breweries, its bland insistence on its own virtue, its explosive homelessness and ethnic cleansing. Portland is easy for me to get to and easy to get my bearings in.

Going to Portland is also a good excuse to go visit with my old pal John Washington. I've spent a lot of time with him over the years, and he never fails to both surprise and delight me. He hasn't really changed all that much; he's just more of the same—but that same is straight gold.

This time, he comes strolling up MLK Boulevard. Black hoodie, black pants, black ball cap and black sunglasses, even though it's a murky March day that's somewhere between rainy and densely misty. His swagger has some shuffle in it now, given the accretive wear-and-tear on his ex–pro football player's body. And possibly, the few extra pounds he's added aren't helping, but *you* tell him that.

John's a great friend and someone I rely on often. He was a star of *What a City Is For*. When I was trying to understand the Albina neighborhood in the north-northeast of Portland and how it was radically gentrified, no one explained that situation as cogently and fiercely as John.

Starting with the 1990 Albina Community Plan—a classic piece of racial cleansing/blight removal/urban renewal legislation—the City of Portland and the Portland Planning Commission very deliberately and effectively cleared Black people out of the one neighborhood in the city they had historically settled. It didn't take long: by 2010 Albina had gone from almost 75 percent Black to less than 25 percent Black, and in the decade-plus since, that percentage has continued to fall. And of course, it is not just homes but Black-owned businesses that have found themselves unwelcome and marooned.

It is important, though, to understand the displacements in Albina not as an aberration, but as part of a larger set of processes. The same logics and worldviews that violently cleansed Indigenous nations from the territory have given permission for the state to make Black people constantly unwelcomed. Oregon has one of the most racist state constitutions in the nation, and non-whites have been actively and violently driven away. When Black people started migrating north during World War II, they were largely confined to Vanport (a portmanteau of Vancouver, Washington, and Portland, Oregon, sister cities facing one another on either side of the Columbia River), a purpose-built war-production camp that opened in 1942.

Vanport soon grew into the country's single largest public housing project, with 42,000 residents at its highest point (including 40 percent Black people), making it Oregon's second biggest city at the time. Located on southern edges of the Columbia River on sweetly productive floodplain, Vanport included hospitals, schools, colleges, movie theaters and shopping centers—a complete and thriving community that had no intentions of disappearing after the war. In 1948, however, the Columbia flooded catastrophically—maybe a natural disaster or maybe one manufactured through negligent flood management and political neglect. Fifteen people died, and the community was functionally washed away. More than a thousand Black families escaped into the city of Portland, where real estate agents, redlining, area councils, politicians and local yahoos made certain that these arrivals were welcomed only in Albina, constraining and constricting their movement to this one neighborhood.

The construction of a new sports complex and the Emmanuel Hospital at the south end of Albina, and then the giant

I-5 highway along its western edge, further squeezed residents so that by 1960, four of five Black Portlanders lived in one 4.3-square-mile area of Albina. When urban renewal arrived, under the guise of evictions, property condemnations, felony restrictions, bylaws and council orders, it easily swamped the neighborhood, displacing and dispossessing residents in the name of urban improvement and uplift.

The story of Albina is both an awful and common story, one that every city can tell in some fashion, but it's also really important not to turn it into a simple victim narrative. Black people were often pushed out of the neighborhood, but everyone was also making rational and reasonable decisions based on available evidence and resources. In the face of relentless racism and pressure, many families, of course, decided to seek calmer pastures, places where white gentry weren't actively leering over their homes, building databases of property values and starting twee little businesses on every block. And this thing's not over. Albina is hardly Black-owned anymore, but it's still a Black neighborhood. John, his Soul District colleagues and so many other Black activists and organizers aren't taking this shit lying down. There are all kinds of powerful people fighting and resisting, building new homes, founding and supporting Black enterprise, banging on every city door, fighting school closures, and scheming major fight-backs and revivals. Every time there's an important meeting or rally or event, people show up, and god help you if you don't pay attention. Jefferson High School might have seen its first-ever non-majority-Black graduating class, but that's very far from the end of the story.

I spent a ton of time on my book about Portland and Albina. It took me years of hustling, weeks and months wandering around the neighborhood, endless interviews, reading everything I could find. I really tried my damnedest to take that story and nest it within large movements and theoretical interlocutions. But after all that—all that thinking, all that research and talking and writing—it is still amazing to me how myopic I was.

I spent years and a whole book thinking about the massive displacement of Black people out of Albina. And yet, despite all that, it's so strange and embarrassing that I really didn't ask where all those people were displaced *to*.

It wasn't just that I didn't do focused research on the question. Honest to god, I just never really thought about it, which now—especially given my ongoing interest in sub-urbs and peripheralization—seems especially weird. But that curious absence—and absence of curiosity—is not just a symptom of my own intellectual blind spots, but what I think is, for much of the urban studies field, an endemic bourgeois tendency to fetishize certain kinds of spatial formations. As soon as those residents exited from my view, it was as if they just walked off the stage.

Albina is such a good example of simultaneously celebrating rootedness and mobility. There has always been powerful resistance to displacement, and despite so many people leaving, Albina remains a Black community, even if the residential demographics have shifted. We can celebrate the people who have stayed and those who have moved with the same fidelity.

10

So, I went back to Portland and Albina to find out what John thinks of this new line of research and argument I'm pursuing. I wanted to find out where people from Albina have moved or are moving to. I wanted to know what happens next. I wanted to know if this phenomenon I'm seeing in so many other cities bears out there too.

I know—from anecdotal evidence, at least—that people from Albina dispersed mainly east and north, to the Numbers, to Gresham, across the river to Vancouver (Washington), to wherever they could find cheap rent. I'm particularly interested in Gresham because it reminds me so much of Surrey: similar distance from the downtown core, similar spatial vibe, similar reputation. It's also not at all like Surrey: it has about a fifth of Surrey's population (something like 115,000 people), is way, way whiter and is not growing anything like the way Surrey is. But it is definitely a spot that people who first moved to East Portland (generally considered east of Eighty-Second) are now heading to.

Gresham is also marked by atrociously ugly racial violence. In 2016, after a brief fistfight, a proud white supremacist ran down and killed a Black teenager with his Jeep.[41] Despite incidents like this, Gresham is also an increasingly common place for Black people to move to when they are looking for cheap housing. Between 1990 and 2010, right in the midst of that startling wave of gentrification in Albina, the Black population of East Portland grew by 151 percent. As longtime Gresham resident Roberta Tyler put it in 2012: "Places where we could never live—Gresham, East Portland—where no one would rent to us, now we call that 'the new ghetto.'"[42] The problem is that even though Black families have moved en masse, they haven't landed in any specific, cohesive area, and the infrastructure—schools, churches, groceries, hair salons, barbers—hasn't followed. Black students find themselves a small minority in schools, surrounded by white ignorance and hostility, with few institutions to turn to.

I wanted to test my theory that there is something really interesting going on right now, something pregnant and rich that not enough people are paying real attention to. In every city I visit it is common knowledge that poor people can no longer afford to live in "inner cities" and are being pushed to the margins. I think that's worth mourning in lots of ways, but what is more, I think it presents new possibilities, new ways to think about organizing, new kinds of spatial and social possibilities. If we are really interested in a politics from below, then surely the sub-urbs are the place to start.

I want to know what John thinks of this argument. I want to ask him about peripheralization. He has watched and fought decades of expulsions from Albina. He knows what it's like for so many people who have left the neighborhood, who travel long distances to go to school, attend church, hang with friends, wander on Mississippi Avenue. John's generally amenable to the outlines of the situation I describe—we've got a good understanding of each other's politics, talk freely and generally agree with other often. But he's not having my argument this time:

Listen, Hern, why the fuck do you want to look into this? What are you trying to get at here? I can see it, and I know how you work, but I'm not sure where your mind is going with this one.

What I think, Hern, you need to know what is driving all of this. What the fuck do you care about suburbs for? It's all the same thing. You need to be asking, what is driving this conduct? Who cares *where* people are getting moved to? Of course they are getting pushed out! That's not interesting—rich white people and their government will do whatever they can with Black people—they will push them here, there or wherever. Where they go doesn't matter. What you need to study is the underlying rationales for this behavior!

Why the fuck do white people act like this?

Over the years, I've gotten used to John's conversational style
—even learned to love it. As we are getting into it, he will typically start a point reflectively and slowly, then hit the accelerator,
rapidly gaining speed and energy, his voice rising as he makes
a point, his huge, meaty hands waving and banging the table,
fingers jabbing at me. He makes points circuitously and complexly, blistering with intensity, disorienting my practiced, linear,
point-to-point argumentative predilections.

I ask one question, and *bang!* J. W. is off, hollering in rapid-fire,
wildly profane arcs and stories. I'm immediately lost, I have no
idea where the fuck he is going—did he mishear my question?
But if I hang in there, the picture slowly starts to come clear.
John's erudite and well-read, with a crazy array of experience,
and he will pull all kinds of threads into any conversation. His
arguments will roam far afield, head back, feint convincingly,
slide another story inside the one he's telling, and then hammer
something home. He will give you his opinions and address your
question, but he won't short you. You'll get your answer, and a
whole lot more too.

It makes total sense that John's a former football player. He
retains a powerful physical confidence and presence. Everything
about him is alpha dog. As he is making a point, it is hardly
unusual for him to bellow, in full flight, something like, "My
warrior is right ready to motherfucking wake UP! If you hurt my
kids and cause them pain for no reason, I will fucking kill you
and eat your fucking heart out with a motherfucking spoon!"
He's aggressive, corporeal, absurdly macho, and full of rage. If
you can't hang with his intensity, so be it, he will offer no apol-
ogies for that. He's all that, but he's also gentle and kind and
sweet in ways he might let you see, in bits and pieces over time.
It's really true: J. W. is a lovely, caring person. But he is sure not
taking any shit.

Spending time with John is simultaneously electric and
exhausting. His urgency sometimes makes it feel like he is about
to attack me, then he pulls up, pumps the brakes, chuckles and
says something sweet. I often wonder if he is enraged with me,
my argument, my slow wit. He has been unfailingly generous

with his time and intellect and hospitality over the years, and I have no doubts about our friendship, but that doesn't preclude him from making clear our disagreements, the inadequacies of my analysis, the places I am too soft to think things through clearly.

11

I arrived at John's office—the Soul District headquarters—on a dreary late February morning when the thermometer said it wasn't that cold, but you still felt the chill. We sat and caught up with his colleague and Soul District managing director, Fawn Aberson, then we wandered up MLK to eat Ethiopian food with Sam Lemil.

Sam is a casually sophisticated, cosmopolitan guy who easily drops mention of the time when he lived in the old-but-bougie part of Rome along the Tiber, the years he spent working across North Africa with the UN, and the range of languages that come easily to him. But Sam's for real. He grew up on a farm in pre–civil rights era Georgia, prefers to spend his days fishing and duck hunting, and he is no stranger to dispossession and displacement. He's a gentle man who knows how to move in different crowds. He's also not averse to an occasional scrap, but he's the scalpel to John's hammer. As he puts it: "When I get angry, John goes and beats someone up."

They have the easy vibe of long-term good friends: they tell war stories, chirp each other, call out each other's BS, finish each other's anecdotes, and clearly rely on each other in obvious and subtle ways. When they part ways, they leave with a "I love you, Black man," and you know they mean it. Throughout our conversation, they keep returning to the theme of "generational wealth" as they turn over my thinking about peripheralization in Portland and Sam keeps locating the questions historically:

Look, Black people have always moved and migrated. The first Black people in Portland were porters on the trains who stayed in the Pearl District, then they got pushed up to Mississippi. Then more Black people came down from Vanport, but those folks all migrated from the South. This is all a result of Black precariousness—sure, people are moving, but what's the underlying force? It's housing yes, but beneath that it's always *jobs*. Black people keep moving trying to stay ahead of it. It is always a cycle.

That's a line of argument I'm particularly interested in. I wonder aloud if there is something about these contemporary sub-urban formations that might offer something new, that in light of the past seventy years of postwar displacements we can learn something, maybe break these ongoing cyclical expulsions. But neither John nor Sam sees much hope of that. Instead, we return to a conversation we've retraced for years: John believes that homeownership is the one hope Black people have, the one chance to build generational wealth, to pass something down to kids. I am entirely suspicious, hostile to the whole construct. John hammers home one of his key economic claims:

> We need a long-term plan. We cannot just be constantly responding to one crisis, to one gentrification after another. Black people need the economic base to catch up to every other group in the country. The only interest people really care about is their own.
>
> We have to teach *our* people how to buy houses. How to run our own businesses. We can never rely on anyone else.
>
> If we own our houses and our land, then we can stand our ground.

John knows the counter-argument I'm going to make, and he's ready, but I make it anyway: homeownership is a mirage. There can be no doubt that for some families, owning a house has been a brilliant life raft, but possession is a trap that ultimately ensnares most of us in a deep, festering precarity, pushing all our money to banks and lenders and capital. To my eyes ideas of ownership are a colonial construct—one of the core roots of inequality, a quicksand of false hope. J. W. is ready with his answer, leaning all the way across the table full of food, pointing his fork at me for punctuation, sermonizing with intent:

Listen, Hern! The reality is that white people control land, the banks, the government—so of course they are going to do and go wherever they want—it's insignificant who is going where or why they are going there.

The root cause of all this is *white supremacy*.

Sure, this peripheralization is happening—of course we see it, we've been seeing it for twenty years here. But all this is just one more result of white control of everything.

Until the ongoing trauma of racism and violence can be addressed, this shit is just going to keep on going. And white people aren't going to give us anything out of the goodness of their hearts.

Sam here, he might believe there is some good in white people, but every piece of evidence suggests otherwise.

I want to know which Africans fought the slavers off? How do we win some battles here and now? Can we win with love? I doubt it. Can we win with anger? In my experience, the white man only respects violence—that's the only way to make systemic change.

Because this dream is still a fucking nightmare.

12

The next day we throw Buster—John's goofily rambunctious six-month-old chocolate lab—into the truck and drive to Gresham. John is well acquainted with my dumb requests and is a great host, so we take a circuitous route out there—we start at the Soul District offices in Albina, head straight north down to the edge of the Columbia Slough and turn left, crossing over and then down to the river proper, looping around the historic Vanport site. It takes about thirty seconds to see what made the place so attractive but also so vulnerable to flooding. All along the river, it's just beautiful, low-lying Delta farmland. The clouds have cleared and the ground itself seems to be sparkling, just asking for someone to plant something. We get out and let Buster run along the river as we chuck rocks and look across at Washington State. The river is broad and peaceful, and you just have to walk up top of the levee, make a 180, and that fertile farm smell comes rolling up to greet you.

But it also takes no time at all to see how disastrous a swollen river would be here. Even after all the levees have been reconstructed and made twenty-first-century-safe, if that river rose, it would just swamp everything in no time. The whole Vanport area lies so low and so flat, it would flood instantly.

We get back in the truck and keep following the river east, past the airport, through Wood Village and drop into Gresham from the north, aiming for whatever downtowns might be there. There are none. Just a few areas with a few strip malls crowded together into a bigger mall complex. A few bigger housing developments here and there. One or two splashy new buildings. A couple of spots where larger malls or mall-adjacent developments draw extra traffic.

We drive around for an hour or so. Up and down the main strips, out to one edge, back to another—and it all feels kind of lonely. There are almost no pedestrians. The whole thing is a little bleak and a little untethered. Like so many peripheral zones, there is a visible lack of visibility—so little to see on the street, aside from traffic. There are no coffee shops, hardly anyone hanging around; the houses and commercial zones are all spread out and set back from the street, everything squirreled away—all the classic blights of contemporary suburban landscapes. What really *is* visible, most obviously around the fringes of Gresham, is a lot of pretty rough-looking poverty.

The idea of *in-between cities* has gained some traction in recent years. It is an urbanist morphological descriptor reaching to characterize spatial formations that don't really fit traditional conceptions of city, suburb, town, village and so on. The term is most frequently deployed to describe sub-urban areas that are densifying, developing town centers, have rapid transit nodes or are emerging fitfully out of classic sprawl landscapes. Surrey is a place that often gets called an *in-between city* because it doesn't adhere easily to either city or suburb spatialities.

I'm not really applying the term correctly here, but it keeps coming to mind as we cruise around the edges of Gresham. So much of it feels in between, lost, sort of abandoned, stuck. Gresham itself definitely has that in-between kind of vibe, if you want to think in terms of a linear spatial progression from rural or agricultural community to village to town to city. Like a lot of suburban peripheral zones, it feels caught in the midst of heading somewhere, suspended in that residential zone, putatively desiring a denser urbanism, but unwilling to get there or unsure about it. But the edges of Gresham, the fringes of the fringe, are where the idea keeps coming back to me.

Like most peripheral zones, Gresham doesn't really have edges. It's all kind of mushy and muddled itself, and its fringes are similarly indistinct. But the homeless people are viscerally conspicuous. Portland, like most every American city, is punctuated by homeless encampments big and small, all throughout the city—patchworks of blue and orange tarps surrounded by garbage, creative ensembles of old furniture, barrels and bikes—lining highway interchanges and under overpasses. As you leave the city proper, like everything else these sites are fewer and further between, but those you do find are more in the open and palpable.

All around the margins of Gresham—in brownfields, alongside ditches, in the midst of abandoned developments, edging right up against four-story buildings that appear to be subsidized housing, out there in awkward little chunks of trees—there are presumptively homeless folks. There are several stretches of roads lined with cars and busted-up campers and vans where people sleep. But instead of the packed homeless encampments in Portland like Dignity Village and Right 2 Dream Too (places I've written about in the past), these spots mimic the residential sprawl around them.

It's not unfamiliar. These are kinds of landscapes you see surrounding cities all over the world in favelas, squats, shantytowns and Traveller and Roma camps. People are moving into wastescapes—abandoned zones where development has failed or never really got traction, the fringe of the fringes. Alan Berger speaks of "drosscapes," zones of urban dereliction, where planners have given up on or given over to low-level or vernacular, unregistered, unofficial, unpermitted development to do what they will, areas left over for whoever to take whatever they can.[43]

The use of "dross" irritates me for some reason; it lands with a kind of pomposity, betraying the bourgeois gaze that urban designers inevitably cast on places they want to "fix." It is absolutely true that Gresham, and even more piercingly at its fringes, does feel left over, abandoned, sort of unstable and unsettling. But I strenuously want to avoid the reflexive, judgy urban clichés that I can so easily revert to.

I hate it so much when people talk shit about Surrey, describe it with "geographies of nowhere" language, can't see anything of value in it, think of it as wasteland, refuse to acknowledge its value. So, I'd better not do it with Gresham.

One way to avoid getting struck in aesthetic distaste for suburbia is to return to thinking though capital and land production.

Fringes can be viewed as landscapes of waste and excess, written off as losses, part of the production of profit, to be returned to whenever there might be a little surplus value squeezed out. John helps me on this:

> You can't separate gentrification and employment. People come here following jobs. As cities deindustrialize, there are all kinds of low-level service jobs out here. This is where they can afford places to rent no matter where they work, but it is also accessible to their places of employment.
>
> You also have to take into account the limits of public transport. You can map the flight from Portland—or anywhere—by mapping public transport. People go as far as buses will take them.
>
> This displacement is all systemic—I studied urban planning and it's one of the first things they taught us. This is all a planned agenda, Hern.
>
> There are no mistakes here—what is the purpose of this round?

This is of course correct and gets me back on track. As we are driving, John is pointing out places where he used to hunt and fish. Places that are now semi-developed, semi-agricultural, semi-residential, and I wonder how a sub-urban set of arguments work for thinking about the other-than-human world. Just as I am musing on that, J. W. pulls the truck up sharply and points: two young deer cross over the road right in front of us, leaping like rainbows over an old, busted-down barbed-wire fence. John smiles and pauses for a long minute, watching as they bounce across a field and disappear behind a trailer park.

> I know where you want to head, Hern. And yes, maybe we can learn from past displacements and yes, maybe there is something here. But the inescapable, key point is this: the place does not matter. *White people don't care where it is*—inner-city, suburb, farm, wherever—as long as they are in control of the wealth and decisions.
>
> There is just so much trauma in Black communities and bodies. We are so used to feeling inferior, less than, like it's our fault, like we are inadequate.

We think we can and will just get pushed out of anywhere, and we'll just take it. Move on.

But we have to fight through that and learn.

My football education tells me that you have to study your opponent. I want to study these white motherfuckers so I can learn their ways and never let them win again.

13

The next day, I take John's suggestion and go back to Gresham on my own to visit the WinCo Foods over on Southeast First Ave, located in a swamp of big-box franchises that include Michaels, Fred Meyer, Olive Garden and O'Reilly Auto Parts. WinCo is a cut-rate grocery store chain popular for the prices, and, well, the prices. I wander in looking for some snacks, and get momentarily stuck in the entrance, a little stunned by the aggressive lighting system and ultra-pastel color scheme.

Extremely unexpectedly, someone recognizes me standing there blinking in the light—it is someone whom I know from years past in Albina. Jasmine is visiting her mom in Gresham. She does not live in Portland anymore, but has moved even further out, further east, past Gresham to Mt. Hood. She does not want me to use her real name because she moved for a job in one of the massive weed-growing operations that have taken over farms all throughout the state. Marijuana is legal in Oregon and there are a ton of growers that export it to states where it is not, but the whole industry still has a semi-outlaw reputation. Any marijuana farm or processing facility is constantly vulnerable to theft, and growers are rarely eager to call the cops, so they all tend to stay pretty much on the down-low, with generic signs out front, some animals wandering around and locked gates.

Jasmine and I go out for coffee at a nearby Starbucks to catch up. I am thrilled to have someone to talk to about Gresham and (of course) overenthusiastically pepper her with questions, wondering if any of my thinking makes sense to her. Fortunately, Jasmine is both patient and excited to talk about suburbs because she too is a little baffled about where she has found herself. She was born and raised in Albina, was surrounded by Black culture and people, never had to own a car, and never really imagined that she would leave. But now she's thirty-three with a big laugh on a hair trigger. She's theatrically nervous about the little strands of gray showing up at her temples, and says she thinks she loves it out in Mt. Hood, mostly because it's easily the most stable and fulfilling job she has ever had. The money is good, the housing is cheap, and the pace relaxed; there's room for her dogs to run around and she says she feels like she has escaped. She only occasionally goes back into Albina, or Portland even—maybe every couple of weeks, just for events or shows or to see friends. Her family is pretty much all out in the burbs now too, so they always gather out here, cousins and kids often showing up for barbeques in her giant backyard, which has a firepit and fruit trees.

It's Sunday morning and Jasmine has to go pick up her mom from church. Her mother used to go back into town religiously on weekends to attend every service at the Emmanuel Church, but now, tired of all the driving, she just goes to a place in Gresham. I tag along and am delighted at how much this new church reminds me of Surrey. It is in a tiny storefront on something of a pedestrian street, sort of a mini-strip-mall thing, one of many low-rise plaza developments lining both sides of the four-lane road. On one side of the church is a nail salon. On the other side is an overseas money-transfer place, a fried-chicken joint, and a cleaners.

We jump out to wade into a small crowd exiting the building and find Mrs. Jackson. The church seems largely Filipino (maybe?). There are definitely some Black people here too, and the vibe is highly convivial, with a church lady at the door passing out bottles of some kind of minerally supplemented water to everyone as they leave. I happily accept one and notice that I am definitely one of the youngest people here. The parking lot is a slow-dancing beehive of cars, and a highly unscientific survey suggests to me that there are a lot of children and grandchildren coming to pick up older churchgoers, many of them playing highly inappropriate music at several volumes too loud. I get a ride to the bus stop. Mrs. Jackson catches my eye and pointedly invites me to stay later for dinner, which I have to decline as I need to be back in the city for an engagement, but I feel sad about that. Mrs. Jackson sighs in a way that suggests she both really wishes I could stay and is pretty relieved I can't.

That little plaza hardly looked anything like what bourgeois urbanism claims as good urban design (read: European), but in practice it displayed all the best characteristics of what a city is supposed to be for. The form and function were disjointed, which is part of why it is such a sweet spot to me. Urban theory (some of mine included) fetishize morphological questions about what a city is, where the urban starts and ends, where to draw city boundaries, what is the right scale of housing, how high streets should be designed, and whether the urban is itself a correct object of study. Those are all important, but second-order, questions. It does not matter how pretty, or well-designed, or walkable any place is if it those attributes are vehicles of dispossession and eviction. In fact, there is almost inevitably a correlation between physical urban attractiveness and whitewashing displacements. Just being at that shitty little plaza/strip mall lifted my spirits. It did not adhere to anything like my ideal of the urban—kind of the opposite, really—but it felt almost perfect. The relationships, sometimes correlative but often causal, between design and displacement are precisely what so many urban planners and designers miss, or more likely just don't give a fuck about.

Maybe that's just the sound of my dogmatic, pissed-off self. But I cannot shake the instinctual feeling that there is something about these new sub-urbanizations, something that offers new chances, new opportunities here. It's not just affordability.

That's obviously the main thing. People move to these new peripheralized zones in search of jobs and affordable housing, a little sense of relief—but maybe more. I'm thinking of John's argument that the place itself is essentially irrelevant—it's just always white supremacy, in this case reproducing itself in the built form. Maybe I too am missing the damn point. I mostly agree, but still, I cling to the idea that the form, the land, the physical, still matters. Is there anything here in the built, material form that lends itself to resistance? If people can escape statist control in a Zomian upward mobility, what about the idea of movement as a kind of refusal in itself?

That argument made some sense to me in Gresham, with people fleeing the racial cleansing of an inner-city neighborhood, but wanted to try somewhere else, to look from another direction. I was looking for a sub-urb that has seen tidal population shifts from basically all white to all Black. I was curious about how that might inflect thinking about peripheries and cities alike, and ideas about social movements and community organizing. So, I decided to visit Ferguson—somewhere I read plenty about but never really imagined spending time in.

14

It doesn't look like all that much, honestly. It's just a place. Nothing here feels all that menacing or fraught, at least not at first glance. It just looks like any sub-urbanish zone on the edge of a big city. I'm not sure if I was anticipating anything in particular, but it's just a store, a plaque in the ground, a busy four-lane road, some semi-desultory business frontages, and a dense mist of history.

I've made my way to Ferguson, Missouri, just outside the city of St. Louis, to think about safety. I spent a chilly March afternoon walking up and down Florissant Avenue (the West, North and South renditions—there is a tangle of Florissants out here). It was here that the riots started in 2014. I stopped at the Ferguson Market & Liquor store, then walked up to Canfield Drive and turned the corner, tracing a teenager's last steps, looking for remnants of the riots that marked the first time almost any of us had ever heard of Ferguson. Images from those days are seared into our minds in precise detail, and yet at the same time lost in the ocean of white-cop-on-Black-youth violence, just one more incident of barbarism among so many others.

In August 2014, Darren Wilson, a white police officer, shot and killed an unarmed Michael Brown. The murder set off weeks of violent protests, triggered again in November of the same year when a grand jury decided not to indict Wilson. Then, in March 2015, the federal Justice Department released a blistering report, calling on Ferguson to completely overhaul its criminal justice and policing systems. The report detailed so many constitutional violations in Ferguson—from police consistently deploying racial slurs and insults, to stopping and cuffing people with no cause, to tasering individuals without provocation—that it recommended abandoning the city's entire policing apparatus, retraining its employees, and establishing new oversight mechanisms.

I am pretty sure you remember all this. You saw all the coverage on TV, heard all the predictable takes and analysis, and glumly presumed that very little was going to change, adding this latest incident to the record of traumatic state-sanctioned racial violence. The endemic failures of the American police state have been documented in granular detail, and those riots felt entirely reasonable, a worthy response to constant threat and degradation and harassment.

It was surprising to many of us to learn that Ferguson is a small, working- and middle-class suburb of St. Louis. That's not really the typical arena where we have come to expect this kind of unrest to explode. Ferguson is not inner-city Detroit or Chicago, it's not the Bronx or South Central—it's just a plain, Midwestern inner-ring suburb of twenty-one thousand people going about its business.

But Ferguson is coldly emblematic of the structural forces that are reshaping American cities—and so many cities everywhere—manufacturing new forms of segregation and marginalization, using new sets of judicial, planning and administrative tools. As Richard Rothstein of the Economic Policy Institute put it in a 2014 EPI report called *The Making of Ferguson*:

> Observers who had not been looking closely at our evolving demographic patterns were surprised to see ghetto conditions we had come to associate with inner cities now duplicated in a formerly white suburban community: racially segregated neighborhoods with high poverty and unemployment, poor student achievement in overwhelmingly black schools, oppressive policing, abandoned homes, and community powerlessness.
>
> Media accounts of how Ferguson became Ferguson have typically explained that when African Americans moved to this suburb (and others like it), "white flight" followed, abandoning the town to African Americans who were trying to escape poor schools in the city. The conventional explanation adds that African Americans moved to a few places like Ferguson, not the suburbs generally,

because prejudiced real estate agents steered black homebuyers away from other white suburbs. And in any event, those other suburbs were able to preserve their almost entirely white, upper-middle-class environments by enacting zoning rules that required only expensive single family homes, the thinking goes.

No doubt, private prejudice and suburbanites' desire for homogeneous affluent environments contributed to segregation in St. Louis and other metropolitan areas. But these explanations are too partial, and too conveniently excuse public policy from responsibility. A more powerful cause of metropolitan segregation in St. Louis and nationwide has been the explicit intents of federal, state, and local governments to create racially segregated metropolises.[44]

Rothstein charts the explicit, public and highly articulated governmental policies that have created path-dependent and entrenched segregated settlement patterns: zoning laws that excluded Black residences and segregated public housing built over once-diverse inner-city neighborhoods; property deeds that prevented the sale of white property to Black residents; tax exemptions for segregation-promoting private institutions, denial of municipal services to Black neighborhoods; redlining; urban renewal projects that destroyed inner-city Black communities. All of these publicly deployed state mechanisms have prevented Black residents from accruing wealth and stability. To quote again from Rothstein's report:

> When we blame private prejudice, suburban snobbishness, and black poverty for contemporary segregation, we not only white-wash our own history but avoid considering whether new policies might instead promote an integrated community.
>
> The federal government's response to the Ferguson "Troubles" has been to treat the town as an isolated embarrassment, not a reflection of the nation in which it is embedded . . .
>
> I do not mean to imply that there is anything special about racial history in Ferguson, St. Louis, or the St. Louis metropolitan area. Every policy and practice segregating St. Louis over the last century was duplicated in almost every metropolis nationwide.[45]

Rothstein's fixation on "integrated" neighborhoods seems pretty dated, something that an older white progressive might predictably aspire to, but then I visited St. Louis. Driving around the metropolitan area—even after a pretty rigorous study of maps and a lot of reading about the city's spatial patterns—I was bewildered by the overt segregation. Almost every place I entered was either all white (with all-Black servers and workers) or all Black. I heard it said a few times that St. Louis feels like it got stuck in the 1960s or early '70s and that the Ferguson unrest was a delayed reckoning that so many other places underwent fifty years ago. I do not know about that, but I paid attention after the third time someone dropped that line.

I got a room downtown, and, hoo boy, that urban depopulation thing that I was warned about is a real thing. The City of St. Louis has been experiencing a sharp and unceasing population decline since 1950, a demographic high point, when it boasted 850,000 people and was the eighth-biggest city in the country. Since then, St. Louis has lost 64 percent of its population(!), with only Detroit and Youngstown experiencing similar collapses. As of this writing, less than three hundred thousand people live in the city, approximately the same population that it had in 1870.[46] The larger metropolitan area, however, has inversely reflected the city's decline, steadily adding population to its current two-and-a-half million: the metro area now has a population close to ten times that of the city proper.

The inner city is eerily empty morning, noon, and night and has an embarrassing, awkward vibe to it—like when you go to a party a little too early and there's no one there, except no one ever really shows up. There's a convention center, a lacing of enormous highways, a stadium, the (unexpectedly very cool) Gateway Arch, some terrible, touristy smokehouse-type restaurants, a few lackluster, try-hard luxury condos, but also a shocking number of abandoned buildings. Big ones. Beautiful Beaux-Arts edifices, like the Orpheum Theater, and the enormous Railway Exchange are all boarded up. Missouri's biggest building by area, the 1.4 million-square-foot AT&T tower, is completely vacant and has been for a long time now.

I walked past the old courthouse (also closed for renos) and was reminded that the Dred Scott case—widely understood to be the worst judicial decision in the history of the United States, which deemed that Black people were not and could never be US citizens—was first heard here in 1847. The urbanist nerd in me insisted that that I visit the iconic Pruitt–Igoe housing site, perhaps the most written about, most studied and most cata-strophic example of urban renewal via segregated public housing, where more than ten thousand people once resided in thirty-three eleven-story towers on a fifty-seven-acre project. The whole thing was mercifully torn down in 1976 after two short decades, and the site just off North Jefferson remains substantively empty, despite never-ending plans for rejuvenation.

What *is* flourishing right next door to the Pruitt–Igoe ruins, on an adjacent, long-empty parcel, is the new, massive National Geospatial-Intelligence Agency West facility (or Next NGA West), a monstrous, creepy-looking campus with a reputed price tag north of $2 billion, where eventually more than three thousand people will be working on "combat support" or, according to the NGA website, producing "world-class geospatial intelligence that provides a decisive advantage to policymakers, warfighters, intelligence professionals and first responders."[47] The whole thing sounds so next-level terrible that I quickly truncated my research about the place, but all the tensions and hostilities and narratives of safety contained on just those two sites kind of shook me.

I met with Julia Ho—a young organizer active in racial justice and solidarity economics movements who, in an unexpected twist, makes her money as a real estate agent, property investor and landlord. She knows the city's housing and displacement patterns as well as anyone and cautions me that St. Louis is a unique case, buffeted by the unabated, steady depopulation of the city core and the resultingly fractured ways gentrifications and evictions are realized. She lives in South City in the hipster neighborhood of Benton Park, home to record stores, vintage clothing shops, and cat cafés, and notes that while people are certainly getting pushed out of there, south to Dutchtown, Mount Pleasant and further, it is not just simple peripheralization. It's more complex and unpredictable than that.

The "Delmar Divide" is the classic way to describe St. Louis—it is 95 percent Black north of Delmar Boulevard and two-thirds white south of it—but data like that, Julia explains, does not account for St. Louis County, which surrounds the city to the west, south and north, with the whole assemblage nestled right up against the Illinois border, meaning that East St. Louis, for example, is not even in Missouri; it's in Illinois. As a result, statistics of all kinds are always manipulated to bolster political positions, with the city and county data disaggregated or combined to prove different points. This pervasive lack of municipal and political will to look closely at the forms of segregation all around the city and county means that solid demographic data is often difficult to come by and, more often than not, actively obfuscating.

A better way to view St. Louis, Julia says, is to look at the Central Corridor—a strip that runs east–west and encompasses the downtown core, the universities, and a series of major governmental and corporate developments—as the major displacing element, and then to trace residential and job patterns extending from it. But no matter where you look or how you look at it, race and segregation lie behind all of it, without fail. The landscape is wildly fractured, which in part explains how far-right US senator Josh Hawley and Black Lives Matter nurse-activist-pastor-turned-congresswoman Cori Bush can represent the same people. St. Louis is a liberal and historically Democratic city that is governed independently, surrounded by the deep (deeeep) red state of Missouri, which makes for a volatile and fractured political landscape, one that takes some time to even start to figure out.

15

On Sunday morning I got up early and, as I was searching for coffee, walked directly into the maw of what seemed to be a massive Republican gathering, or a Tucker Carlson event or something —I couldn't quite tell. The always-empty downtown streets were absolutely teeming with people, as hordes of cops tried, with only partial success, to direct the crowds. There was just so much beer, and it was all—like really, really *all*—white people.

I was frantically scanning for escape routes, wondering how the hell I had missed the warning signs, and then I figured it out. It was the home opener of the St. Louis Battlehawks, an XFL football team, and 38,000-plus people had come to see the newly revived professional football league. A few years earlier, St. Louis had lost its NFL team to Los Angeles (of all the hurtful places), and the sports-crazed city showed out that morning with a sea of tailgaters swarming every available parking lot from 8 a.m. on, filling stairwells and alleys with rivers of vomit and newly minted chants for their boys.

The avalanche of traffic suggested that all these people had streamed into the city core from the suburban peripheries. They sure were not taking public transit—as usual, the subway was mostly bereft of riders that day. Throughout my stay, I was warned repeatedly to avoid the subway, that it was not safe, that I would likely get repeatedly harassed for money, probably aggressively. I took the train a couple of times, and it seemed fine, but it was covered with signage touting the new Secure Platform Plan, "a multi-tiered plan to grow ridership on the Metro Transit system by creating a more secure transit environment," including new gates, emergency phones, facial recognition technologies, more fencing, more cameras and more security. The company says it is "committed to rebuilding ridership and regaining the region's confidence," which sounds kind of ominous, and the insistence that the trains were safe made me a little anxious.

The logics of suburbia have always been bound up with competing notions of safety and claims about how to best handle real and perceived threats. Ancient cities expelled unwanted residents, forcing them outside the city walls, to live literally beneath the *urb*. Wealthier people have always been able to escape the crowded confines of cities to safe havens where they can enjoy fresh air and quiet surroundings while maintaining easy access to city comforts. The modern suburb, though, only emerged through the Industrial Revolution via the development of mass transit technologies—it was trolley and rail lines first, then the private automobile, that gave wheels to the dream of escape.

The Victorian city, with all its hazardous housing, crime, overcrowding, deplorable hygiene, and class volatilities, birthed the notion of the countryside as a safe haven, a safety hatch for anxious urbanites. But that version of safety has always been captured by the gravitational force of racial paranoias, animated by private prejudice, institutional conniving and segregationist public policy. During the great American postwar suburban build-out, the Federal Housing Administration wildly subsidized the construction of iconic developments like Levittown, New York, but only on the condition that these new suburbs be made exclusively available to white people through restrictive covenants in combination with redlining and the denial of insurance for Black families. This overt, systematic segregation left inner cities with huge concentrations of low-income Black families coping with a deepening cycle of the withdrawal of social services funding and declining tax bases, meaning worsening schools, fewer jobs, and rising crime rates.

This story of forced movement, displacement and urban reordering is tiresomely familiar to all of us: we all just presume that wealthier, whiter residents will move en masse, like migrating flocks of birds, either out of or back into the city, and force everyone else to adjust around them. Rothstein's argument is that we should see all of this not just as the expression of individual or cultural prejudice, but as an overt set of government policies that create segregation. He is certainly correct, but I keep wondering: Then what is behind those government policies? Is it not the logic of white supremacy that drives them? Is it not some kind of ouroboros-esque mess?

Rothstein is convinced that if "we understand that our segregation is a governmentally sponsored system, which of course we'd call *de jure* segregation, only then can we begin to remedy it. Because if it happened by individual choice, it's hard to imagine how to remedy it. If it happened by government action, then we should be able to develop equally effective government actions to reverse it."[48] That kind of faith in government action as a primary driver of change is heartening in some ways, but missing the forest for the trees. The constant deferral to segregation as *unconstitutional*—as something that can be remedied via governmental policy, court challenges and invocations of the United States' supposedly ethical and equitable foundations—seems naive at best. I tend to rely on a very different kind of faith: that only grassroots organizing, active refusal and rebellion drives change; government policy can only react and respond.

As I wound my way in and out of various St. Louis neighborhoods, charting patterns and asking people to explain to me where people are being displaced to, I keep thinking back to Surrey and Portland, keep wondering about other ways to think about displacement. I keep hearing John Washington in my head:

> You need to be asking, what is driving this conduct? Who cares *where* people are getting moved to? Of course they are getting pushed out! That's not interesting—rich white people and their government will do whatever they can with Black people—they will push them here, there or wherever. Where they go doesn't matter. What you need to study is the underlying rationales for this behavior! Why the fuck do white people act like this?

I think John's point is correct, but at least right now, I'm not all that personally confident about trying to figure out those underlying rationales. I am on much surer ground thinking about action and responses, so I called up Colin Gordon, who is the author (among many other books) of *Citizen Brown: Race, Democracy and Inequality in the St. Louis Suburbs* and *Mapping Decline*, to get a better sense of the kinds of peripheralizations that created St. Louis and the carceral conditions that incubated the Ferguson riots. He explained:

> Ferguson is an inner-ring, black-flight "secondhand" suburb. The larger logic of racial segregation in the metro area is (or was) replicated on a smaller scale in Ferguson—especially in the divide between single-family homes in the north and multifamily south towards Maline Creek. It is positioned north of a stable racial boundary (the "Delmar Divide" that extends out from the city) and in the midst of an unstable one (the zone of racial transition moving east to west across the county).
>
> This sustains, as you suggest, a persistent spatial mismatch between residential and economic opportunity—first marked by the hollowing out of the central city, then by the steady suburbanization of investment and employment. The compound tragedy of this is both that segregation and disadvantage move with the African American population to the (inner) suburbs, but that everything (employment, public goods, access to social services) is thinner in suburban settings.

I spent at least part of every day I was in St. Louis hanging around Ferguson, and often sitting in a booth at Cathy's Kitchen on Florissant, where I got multiple earfuls about the city. Every time anyone talked about Ferguson, they also wanted to tell me about Kinloch.

Ferguson used to be essentially all white. It was a sundown town right up until the late 1960s, where Black people were banned after dark. In 1970 the population was 99 percent white and perhaps 1 percent Black, if that. That percentage has now been reversed: in 2000, it was 52.4 percent Black and 44.7 percent white, and by 2020 it was 72 percent Black and only 21 percent white. But back when it was an all-white town, Black people lived in Kinloch, the next town over, and commuted to Ferguson to work as nannies, cooks and cleaners. At sundown, Ferguson would draw a chain across the road and block it with vehicles and garbage. But there was no chance Black people wanted to be there after dark anyway; it was highly dangerous, so people stayed in Kinloch, where "they felt safe in the confines of the town in ways they didn't outside the town."[49]

In the 1980s the City of St. Louis started buying up property in Kinloch. Lambert airport was expanding, and an FAA noise-abatement requirement meant that the town was in the way and needed to be dispersed. Between 1990 and 2000 Kinloch lost more than 80 percent of its population, dropping from 2,700 to 450, and what was once a thriving, welcoming, and vibrant little place descended into a crime-ridden town mostly filled with ghosts. Census data says 263 people live there as of 2022, but when I drove around, I kept stopping to check my directions. There really was no there *there*—it was block after long country block grown over with vegetation, most of which looked like an open-air dump. Thousands upon thousands of mattresses were strewn everywhere; there were hundreds of old cars and appliances, millions of bags of garbage, and a house here and there that may have been inhabited.

Eventually, I found a city hall perched on a scraggly little hill in the far corner of the city overlooking the airport, looking tidy but locked. Nearby was a fire station, and then on the opposite far corner of the city there was a single housing project, bounded by high fences that looked like maybe a couple of hundred people could live there. The whole thing was disquieting and weird, and when I asked my table at Cathy's about Kinloch, everyone looked alarmed that I had gone there, even in my rented SUV, even when I assured them that I had kept my doors locked. "That used to be the best place, son. Now it's the worst." A statewide commission appointed by the governor in 2015 in the wake of the Michael Brown shooting found that the average lifespan in Kinloch was more than thirty years less than those living in the nearby, mostly white suburb of Wildwood.[50]

16

In 2020 Congresswoman Alexandria Ocasio-Cortez was one of a handful of progressive legislators speaking out against police abuse. In an online forum that summer, she responded to a question about the defund movement: "When people ask me, 'What does a world where we defund the police look like?', I tell them it looks like a suburb."[51]

Everyone understood what she meant, but she also chose a lousy example. Police now kill far more people in suburbs than cities, and even by 2016, for the first time in US history, arrest rates in suburban cities were higher than in their principal cities, as revealed by the Vera Institute of Justice's interactive Arrest Trends tool: "The difference between police treatment of Black people and white people in suburban cities continues to worsen just as suburbs become more diverse with a growing Black and Latino middle class."[52]

Between 2014, the year of Michael Brown's shooting, and 2022, St. Louis led the nation in murder rate overall, and the St. Louis Metropolitan Police Department (SLMPD) has the highest rate of police killings by population of any police department of the one hundred largest US cities according to 2021 data recorded by ArchCity Defenders.[53] In 2023 St. Louis was once again named the least safe city in America, and there are few reasons to think these trajectories will be altered any time soon.[54]

The month before I arrived in Ferguson, the Missouri House of Representatives rejected a proposal that would have required children who openly carry firearms to do so only with the permission of their parents. Missouri residents currently do not need a concealed-carry permit, nor do they have to take safety training or have a criminal-record check to carry a gun in most public places. As Republican state representative Bill Hardwick put it: "I just have a different approach for addressing public safety that doesn't deprive people, who have done nothing to any other person, who will commit no violence, from their freedom."[55] I did think about this every time I walked into a bar or met someone new, and I did notice the signs in many establishments requesting people not to open carry.

The month before the rejection of that ban, the same House passed a revised dress code that requires women legislators to cover their arms when in the chamber.[56] This revision was driven by the same group of people who fought tooth and nail against any mask-wearing requirements during the pandemic. The men's dress code was not addressed.

All of this was definitely on my mind as I tried to find my way around Ferguson, but that's not what I am really after here. I am most interested in thinking about how we think about suburbia —and by extension, cities—and trying to dispense with all the paternalism and myopia and clichés that occlude a clear conversation. AOC is wonderful, but that kind of throwaway comment is decidedly unhelpful. Certainly some suburbs are very safe for some people, but that's not everyone, and many sub-urbs—maybe most of them—are markedly unsafe, especially for low-income and racialized people.

To talk about cities and suburbs is always to talk about safety, but it is an intensely politicized idea, and what feels safe for one person may well be highly dangerous for another. Some people argue that an increased police presence equals more safety, while for others, the notion of more cops is terrifying. Think about every argument you know of that roots itself in safety claims—whether it is about guns, cameras, guards, laws, cars, surveillance or whatever—and more safety for one group always means less for another.

Just as with the social determinants of health, safety is also a constructed notion, and thus it's something we can argue about. It's statistically true that many modern suburbs are not so safe (if we are measuring violent crime, murders and arrests), but that obviously changes drastically depending on who and where you are. I love the idea that having more people around, that eyes on the street creates a safer environment. I believe that a vibrant public milieu, front porches, life lived outside, is far safer than people locking themselves away in their houses behind militarized defenses. I have long believed that cities are inherently safer than suburbs—but for whom?

One Saturday in St. Louis, I went to the ArchCity Defenders office downtown and attended a training session for organizers interested in police abolition and defunding. ACD is a tremendous organization, devoted to combatting "the criminalization of poverty and state violence, especially in communities of color [via] legal representation, social services, impact litigation, policy and media advocacy and community collaboration," and the session was genuinely moving, with mothers of slain children speaking frankly, and people sharing all kinds of stories about the failures and cruelty of the legal, police and incarceration apparatuses.

The workshop was split into two parts. The first covered the history and evolution of policing, including its origins in America in the form of white militias or slave patrols convened for tracking down fugitive, escaped slaves: these were vigilante groups protecting and disciplining white property. Then, after the Civil War, white segregationists regrouped as part of widespread retaliation against the end of slavery, regaining political power in every southern state via voter repression and intimidation, and creating formal police departments across the nation to enforce Jim Crow laws. Through the late nineteenth century and early decades of the twentieth century, police mandates aggressively expanded their reach to suppress labor movements and social organizing, all in the name of defending white power and property, which remains the central goal of carceral systems.

The second part of the workshop focused on thinking about practical routes to abolition in material terms. On some level it seems confounding to even imagine a world beyond policing and prisons and surveillance, but in many ways it's not hard at all. Almost everything police are currently tasked with can be done better, more effectively and more humanely by other people, and we would all be so much better off if people's needs were attended to rather than disciplined. To those who cling to the idea that police and prison culture is effective, or can be reformed, I'd only ask: How's that working out so far? Given the accelerating and multiplying effects of what Mariame Kaba calls "death-making institutions," from prisons to policing to borders, it is surely time to get more creative and more urgent about finding better kinds of safety. Kaba writes:

> People like me who want to abolish prisons and police, however, have a vision of a different society, built on cooperation instead of individualism, on mutual aid instead of self-preservation. What would the country look like if it had billions of extra dollars to spend on housing, food, and education for all? This change in society wouldn't happen immediately, but the protests show that many people are ready to embrace a different vision of safety and justice. When the streets calm and people suggest once again that we hire more Black police officers or create more civilian review boards, I hope that we remember all the times those efforts have failed.[57]

If we know that displacements and peripheralizations are creating a fractured and dislocated landscape of suburbia and sub-urbias, and if we see that so many collective refusals and revolts are happening far from city centers—whether in Ferguson or Rinkeby or Bairro da Jamaica or Tregear or banlieues or wherever—then what new routes might that knowledge offer in thinking about reimagining safety?

One of the things I noticed often in St. Louis, and especially in Ferguson, is that despite people's quick-draw eagerness to enumerate the city's long list of failings and embarrassments, there was a simmering pride and loyalty. The whole of St. Louis seems to be a place you could defend fiercely in the same breath that you decry how fucked up it is. I know this kind of protectiveness. Despite my dismay at basically every institution and built feature of Surrey, I have become basically an at-large chamber of commerce, some kind of weird civic booster, ready to drop the mitts with the first outsider who says anything ill about the place.

I keep thinking that this kind of pride and fidelity might offer something new, something to celebrate and to find new ways to think about safety. I am hopeful that these new sub-urban forms, in all their mess and unsettledness, might offer novel ways to revolt and remake, to find different ways to keep us safe, and to realize Kaba's call for "a million experiments"—a sea of new initiatives and projects and institutions to replace carceral violence.

Not long after that workshop, I met with Inez Bordeaux, a community organizer and abolition activist. She works almost exclusively in the city and spoke about how complicated it is to operationalize her work in the North County, even though that's where the vast majority of people in the metro area live. The county has eighty-eight separate municipalities, and they are wildly different from one another: some are wealthy, white and Republican, while some, like Ferguson, are majority Black with very high concentrations of poor, unhoused and marginalized people. Organizing in the county is super complicated because there are so many different jurisdictions, all with their own police, their own laws, and their own judges and legal systems. I asked Inez what effect Ferguson and the protests have had on these places and the region as a whole:

> The sustained, year-long protests in Ferguson certainly were not the first time this sort of thing had happened, but people in Ferguson were so loud and so bright that they acted as a kind of beacon, a kind of North Star for this whole new generation of organizers who have said we're not taking this shit anymore; we're going to start from the ground up and we're going to build the St. Louis that we all deserve.
>
> A lot of the positive changes we are seeing here started in Ferguson. There is a wave of amazing, powerful people and organizations who have returned and emerged here because of what happened in 2014. I can go on and on and on about the folks who are changing this city and the way we think about public safety and policing and because of Ferguson. Ferguson. I think it started there. So much brilliant social justice work was already here before that, but so many positive reforms just didn't

exist before Ferguson. That's a fire that continues to burn bright for all of us. All of it stems from Ferguson. I'd love for someone to prove me wrong, but I know I'm right.

I'm not fighting her on that point. Even after just a brief visit, I'm pretty sure she's right.

Part 2

TURNING THE CITY INSIDE OUT

Circulation . . . is the only political stake and the only real space of political struggle.

—Michel Foucault, *Security, Territory, Population*

1

American suburbs have defined a now-globalized fantasy that has infected dreams in every corner of the world: an owner-occupied, single-family lot with a grassy yard, a barbeque grill in the back, and a recent-model vehicle on a sanitized cul-de-sac with a well-funded school within walking distance. We are all intimately familiar with this allusive imagery, but even more intimately we understand the economic, sexual, gendered and racialized relationships it orders. Suburbanism demands fidelity to very specific and explicit ways of being.

There is an active constituency that wants to describe this ordering as "market choice"—claiming that this is how most people want to live, so suburban developers, planners and municipalities simply deliver the goods. This, of course, is as absurd as it is offensive. Contemporary suburbanization has been structured and regulated as spatial expressions of white supremacy in precisely the same ways that segregated core-city neighborhoods have been made and remade. Cities and municipalities have created expansive suburban regimes through a web of collusion made up of real estate and lending practices, racist grassroots movements, zoning policies, infrastructure spending, tax regimes, municipal land ordinances and everyday threats of violence alongside micro-exertions of power, control, fear and exclusion.

Consider just one example: among the most powerful mechanisms for homeownership in US history was a portfolio of federal underwriting programs that, by the 1950s, resulted in one-third of all new homebuyers receiving support from the Federal Housing Administration (FHA) and Veterans Affairs programs alone. These postwar initiatives were so successful that

American homeownership rose from approximately 40 percent in the 1940s to well over 60 percent in the 1960s, with the vast majority of these new owner-occupied dwellings in newly built suburbs. But FHA guidelines officially sanctioned racial segregation until the 1950s, and unofficially enforced it long after that. Thus, by 1960, Black people and people of color had received less than 2 percent of FHA-insured mortgages.[1]

Suburbanism is an allocation argument about how land should be distributed, used and controlled. That argument is articulated by transportation, shopping and public space design, but it is anchored by a deep and abiding commitment to individual homeownership. More than highways, commutes, malls and cul-de-sacs, the suburban fantasia is about property and home-ownership. And in that, it is always an argument about whiteness.

The postwar American suburban construction boom transformed existing notions of who counted as "white," and many different categories of people who had previous been excluded from that designation—Irish, Italians, Jews, Eastern Europeans, Greeks—were brought into the fold. These people had always been thought of as something else, something fluid, and definitely *not white*, but the suburbs and the experiences of World War II allowed for a new set of solidarities. The shared oasis of home-ownership created novel bonds of shared experiences, occupying the newly opened lands of suburbia with reconstituted fidelities.

As Herbert Gans, William Whyte and a long series of observers found when exploring these new landscapes, even the most exclusive and regulated of the new suburbs had significant forms of diversity.[2] Threading through neighbourhood after neighbourhood were more signs of difference along lines of class, religion and politics than most had anticipated. And even in the earliest years of suburbia, this engendered real and living social capital: clubs and associations, backyard collaborations, babysitting collectives, school parent committees, Tupperware parties and sports teams flourished, all contributing to the notion of suburbia as an escape, a new utopian frontier.

But American diversity has always been defined by an allegiance to anti-Blackness, with significant doses of other racialized exclusions: deep anti-Asian sentiment in West Coast suburbs, for example, has been well documented. The suburban commitment to private property is a foundational narrative for articulating new forms of highly gendered and sexualized whiteness, and suburbia is a preeminent form, giving permission and structure to new renditions of very old racist stories. The construction of suburbia gave people, including those newly deputized as white, opportunities to concretize their racial claims through claims to property. As W. E. B. Du Bois put it in 1920:

> I am given to understand that whiteness is the ownership of the earth forever and ever, Amen! Now what is the effect on a man or a nation when it comes passionately to believe such an extraordinary dictum as this? That nations are coming to believe it is manifest daily. Wave on wave, each with increasing virulence, is dashing this new religion of whiteness on the shores of our time.[3]

Land is the first commodity, and new suburban developments transform non-valuable, stagnant rural, agricultural and unused land immediately into property commodity. The explosion of postwar prosperity in the Global North, and especially the United States, was driven by the manufacturing of wealth out of *nothing* land, land that had to be rescued from the "citadel of dead capital," as Hernando de Soto put it, and transformed into property. This is of course the story of settler colonialism, and its suburban expansionism is properly understood as a re-enactment of the settler-colonial drive to capture land from its *terra nullius* torpor via occupation.

It is no surprise, then, that it is in the United States, Canada, Australia and New Zealand where the modern suburban form was birthed and nurtured. Other places try to mimic suburban-ism, and often succeed in patches, but it is in unreconstructed and unapologetic settler-colonial societies where contemporary suburbanism exploded on to the landscape. As Quandamooka scholar Aileen Moreton-Robinson puts it, "It takes a great deal of work to maintain Canada, the United States, Hawai'i, New Zealand, and Australia as white possessions," and suburbia is carrying a heavy workload.[4]

To explain the structural workings of settler-colonial societies, Moreton-Robinson uses the term *possessive logics*, which are "operationalized within discourses to circulate sets of meanings about ownership of the nation, as part of commonsense knowledge, decision making, and socially produced conventions." This set of meanings buttresses a "hegemony, ideology, epistemology, and ontology" of patriarchal white supremacy that "requires the possession of Indigenous lands as its proprietary anchor."[5]

Referencing Cheryl Harris's seminal 1993 *Harvard Law Review* article "Whiteness as Property,"[6] Moreton-Robinson writes: "As a form of property, whiteness accumulates capital and social appreciation as white people are recognized within the law primarily as property-owning subjects."[7] Property and whiteness entangle, and the inverse is equally true: non-whiteness is rightly property-less, and thus suburbia, as a utopian exercise, has to be exclusive. Australian scholar of settler colonialism Lorenzo Veracini describes suburban exclusivity as reenacting settler colonialism. Because both produce "localized sovereign capacities," it is easy to draw parallels: "Settlers and suburbanites are founders of political orders and are especially focused on exercising local control over local affairs."[8]

Like settler-colonial logics, suburban boosters are particularly fond of escape narratives. White anxiety is a prominent feature of both narratives, requiring both a fearful flight to the periphery from a dangerous, cluttered and unstable center and a nostalgic return to "the way things used to be": pastoral, secure, sanitary, unencumbered by racialized newcomers. This is a world made anew in the service of white idealism, and, like all "community" discourses, it requires constant vigilance to defend borders, build moats, and ensure common-sense understandings of what and who is and isn't acceptable.

Much as with settler colonialism, there is now significant destabilization of the suburban ideal, a fraying and unraveling that is increasingly complicated to contain. Borders become permeable, whole chunks fall away, territory is relinquished, doubt and uncertainty creeps in. White anxiety, like capitalist crisis, is never "solved"; it is only moved around. As Veracini writes:

By definition, imagining the world-turned-inside-out requires an outside. But an inexorable law of diminishing returns makes thinking the world-turned-inside-out progressively more and more difficult. The crisis eventually catches up, and the world-turned-inside-out turns inward. Gated communities and a "fortress" mentality endeavour to retain separation but have given up on displacement and have accepted the need to manage propinquity by enforcing separation from anxiety-generating surrounding environments, and the people that live there, in alternative ways.[9]

The spatial fix of suburbia was built by spectacular postwar infusions of both public and private investment, precipitating the still-unfolding convergence of real estate and global financial markets. Beginning in the 1960s as financialization emerged as the dominant mode of contemporary accumulation, every form of capital concentration, from investment banks to pension funds to insurance funds to a fantastic array of exotic investment vehicles, has poured resources into real estate and suburban industrial expansionism. The explosive scale and scope of investment has persisted, nay flourished, enduring recurrent financial and market crises, recessions and instabilities, such that by 2002 the United States was losing two acres of farmland per minute, a rate that increased to three acres per minute by 2018.[10]

That voracious consumption of land meant that somewhere around 1990, the preeminent suburb-building countries—the United States, Australia and Canada—all had become majority suburban, but that designation is of course fraught. No longer is it clear at all where cities start and stop, and it has never been clear what exactly constitutes a suburb, as what is typically designated as such often contains multitudes of shifting forms and patterns. Just as what actually defines a city is ineffable and unstable, naming a suburb is mostly performative.

But what *is* clear is that it is a mess. There are fewer and fewer suburbs that adhere to easy clichés, and so much of what we call classical suburbia is fracturing and restructuring as sub-urbia. Urban peripheries across the globe are becoming increasingly complex and destabilized. As racialized residents acceleratingly breach suburban gates, the center cannot hold, and white people are fleeing to new, urban gated communities downtown— settlements that vertically segregate in condo towers—and displacing and banishing huge swaths of low-income residents who rearrange themselves on messy—and cheaper—urban fringes.

I contend that this is a moment rich with potential: as suburbia disassembles and reorders, it opens up new possibilities for land and property. As the materiality of contemporary sub-urbia consistently fails to articulate the "white possessive," what kinds of fidelity might new sub-urbias nurture?

The answers for me are all affective: being in Surrey feels exciting, as though so much more is in play, released from the certainties of Vancouver's tightly ordered and planned streets, it feels far more complicated, unfamiliar, unpredictable. The edges are always harder to manage, they are always full of barbarian incursions, they are always threatening to slip outside regimes of command and control and thus are always subject to suspicion and derision, but also to uncertainty.

All that messy absence of planning makes many urbanists and planners anxious: there is nothing even vaguely like a "smart city" in Surrey, nor in many sub-urbs. And it is exactly that messiness that offers so many opportunities to unravel narratives of property and ownership. All that sprawl of Surrey is happening on unceded Indigenous territory and I wonder what kinds of possibilities the frothy diasporic layering of Surrey might offer for decolonial narratives. Can sub-urban patterns of displacement and banishment nurture a new politics from below? Is it possible that the uncertainties of the *sub* can trouble the accumulative power of the *urb*?

2

It's not just sub-urbs that are a mess. The way that we understand cities is equally untidy, in part because the notion of "the city" as a clearly bounded, comprehensible entity is increasingly untenable. Political and cartographic lines are performative exercises, and every city overfills its cup, spills over into the countryside, infiltrates neighbor municipalities, swamps its suburbs. The banal, sprawling ubiquity of the contemporary urban form tends to confuse traditional urban scholarship that relies on easy distinctions.

Among the most prominent recent efforts to make sense of metastasizing urban forms is the exhaustively (and exhaustingly) debated "planetary urbanization" thesis, forwarded initially by Neil Brenner and Christian Schmid, but soon piled on by many, many others. The thesis is one among a much larger body of work strongly influenced by the thinking of French philosopher and sociologist Henri Lefebvre, who was writing about "complete urbanization" as early as the 1960s.

The planetary urbanization thesis argues for a "new epistemology of the urban," claiming that the phenomenon of urbanization has simultaneously exploded and imploded, rendering familiar distinctions of city/countryside, urban/rural, society/nature, North/South and so on meaningless. Following Lefebvre, Brenner and Schmid claim that processes of "extended urbanization" have drawn the entire planet into an accelerated capitalist urbanization, with even "hinterlands," "wilderness landscapes" and "remote" areas no longer something distinct, with essentially everything operationalized to service the metabolic desires and needs of urban growth. Thus, Brenner and Schmid have claimed that there "is no longer any outside to the urban": the entire globe has been reduced to extended operational landscapes of urbanization.

This thesis has incited vigorous rounds of debate, and while I think the planetary urbanization argument has some real insights to offer toward undermining cheap binaries, I am always highly suspicious of any thesis that tries to subsume disparate fields of inquiry into a "theory of everything"–style universalizing narrative. I like a lot of the work Brenner and Schmid et al. are doing to try to reconceptualize scopes of urban inquiry, and this thesis, at its best, goes a long way toward opening up our fields of vision, imploring us to look to processes well beyond city walls.

The problem is that planetary urbanization, in its worst renditions, is a totalizing theory that ignores everyday places and processes, dismisses the outside as parochial, and squeezes out relational thinking. At its very worst, extended urbanization goes all theoretical *terra nullius*, emptying out the globe and then remapping it using neocolonial cartographies, extinguishing difference as it goes, barfing global-city theory over all kinds of rich, disparate threads of thinking. As Rajyashree Reddy puts it:

> Rather than fully subsuming the rural into the urban, we must strive for deeper understanding of the urban's many constitutive outsides, including the rural, because they are what allow for radical alterity and radical undecidability . . . within the urban itself.[11]

Winding through all the planetary urbanization debates is a generalized agreement, implicit and explicit, that there are some kinds of thresholds that have been surpassed. The tired claim that the planet is more than 50 percent urban has proven itself functionally useless. It is certain that the comfortable distinctions and binaries that have long driven urban theory are exhausted, that settlement patterns of all kinds are unstable materially and theoretically, that we need new languages to make sense of a world that increasingly fails to adhere to urbanist orthodoxies.

And looming monstrously over all these conversations is the acceleratingly urgent threat of global warming—or, as some have it now, "global heating," or just plain ole "climate catastrophe."

Liberal urbanists tend to view suburbanism as among the primary drivers of climate change specifically, and ecological degradation in general. *Sprawl* is the worst four-letter word in urbanist parlance, an unqualified ill, an embarrassment, a stand-in for bad planning, the driver of metastasizing emissions and, for many, quite possibly the single most damaging set of land-use policies imaginable.

The antidote, then, is density. A generation of progressive urbanists and planners have lionized density as the one amelioratory organizing concept that everyone can agree on. And in some part, I too agree. Density, especially residential density, opens up possibilities for compact, complete communities, walkable neighborhoods, urban vitality and a host of cultural and political virtues that non-car-dependent proximity putatively nurtures. I believe there's a lot that's right with that proposition. The problem with so much of this thinking, however, is that it fractures the analysis into an apolitical set of prescriptions for redevelopment, urban renewal, and an endless parade of dense, numbingly bland, sanitized urban neighborhoods that no one can afford.

Global warming is a desperate problem and reducing emissions dramatically is absolutely necessary. Sprawling suburban development hamstrings any efforts to reduce regional VKTs (vehicle kilometers traveled), and thus density is certainly part of the answer. But in their pursuit of density, urban planners endemically ignore the processes that are driving contemporary sprawl. In clinging to a nostalgic binary that clearly delineates the suburban from the urban, most planners and cities are actively and willfully exacerbating the problems they purport to address.

Almost every attempt to enforce density, via so-called "smart" planning, New Urbanism and all its variants, almost inevitably becomes one more excuse for displacement. In city after city, I have seen new developments that, by adhering to liberal environmental planning orthodoxies, banish residents further afield. Without an aggressive confrontation with inequality, planning for density just ends up replicating and accelerating the same processes of sprawl. Except in this rendition, it comes with an added layer of shame. New forms of sub-urbanization expel low-income and marginalized residents from city cores and then blame them as eco-villains for driving incessantly.

This is of course an old colonial trick. After pillaging Indigenous communities and the Global South for centuries, experts from the Global North now descend on poor communities with condescending prescriptions for fixing the damage done. This is the easily recognizable "development" narrative that gets replicated at the urban scale. As poor, working-class and migrant communities increasingly inhabit sprawling sub-urbia, they are besieged with patronizing environmental opprobrium about the poverty of their "lifestyles." The sub-urbs do not need to be "fixed," and certainly not by the same prescriptions that are turning inner cities into exclusive centers of wealth and privilege.

Suburbia has always been a product of capitalist reordering. New and emerging forms of sub-urbanization have to be understood similarly, as material expressions of capital accumulation and restructuring, displacement and dispossession. Over the past seventy years of explosive economic and population growth, it has been axiomatic that wealth fuels sprawl. Richer cities are vastly less dense than poorer ones. Wealthier people consume more of everything: more services, more land, more goods. That has not, and will not, change—only the form of that consumption shifts. Confronting global warming has to be far more than a facile reading of sprawl—we have to understand the narratives that rest on endless consumption, accumulation and theft. Sub-urbia is just one more result of a set of stories fueled by insatiable hunger.

3

It is not urbanization that has become planetary; it is the processes of displacement and expulsions that have become globally normalized—just business as usual. We are not living under complete urbanization; it is the convergence of banishments—spatial and otherwise—as a way of being in the world that it is so hard to find an outside of.

There is no single globalized sub-urbanism, any more than there was ever a planetary urbanization or planetary suburbanization. We are witnessing a myriad of polycentric, fractured and unstable re-arrangements of urban regions that throws into question everything we know about cities and their regions.

Instead of reaching for the universal, the right route is to focus on the processes that are at play in certain places: the kaleidoscopic exclusions and alienations and displacements that are perpetually excluding certain people from centers of power and legitimacy and mobility. This can reorient the ways we think about the "urban," and perhaps suggests a bottom-up, inside-out set of analyses. New patterns of solidarities, new ways to confront social marginalization, new kinds of gathering spaces, and new ways of living are thriving within sub-urban landscapes, many of which do not adhere to my easy leftist imaginings.

One of Giorgio Agamben's most potent theoretical interventions in recent decades is the idea of *the camp*. Through his work on states of exception, Agamben has called the camp the "nomos of the modern," or "the hidden matrix" of modern life, or the "space that is opened when the state of exception begins to become the rule." Agamben claims that the camp has replaced the city as the biopolitical formation of modern times, represented by places like Auschwitz or Uighur detention facilities or refugee camps or Indigenous reservations or Guantanamo Bay, but also by a vast array of other physical manifestations and structures such as mass incarceration. States of exception are invoked by the sovereign to surpass or exceed the law, to simultaneously make the law and stand outside it, leaving certain people reduced to bare life. Agamben describes an "inclusive exclusion" or "exclusion through inclusion" that structures political relationships, a confinement of certain populations in particular spaces: campsites.

The experience of sub-urbia is constantly inflected with feelings of inclusion/exclusion: feeling that you are outside and refusing it in the same breath. Achille Mbembe holds that the camp form—refugee camps, prisons, banlieues, sub-urbs, favelas—has become a prevailing way of governing unwanted populations, enclosed in precarious spaces so that they can be controlled, harassed and potentially killed. It is a permanent condition of "living in pain," a kind of pain that is compounded by the fact that you know exactly what kind of pain you are in.

The enforcement of biopolitical ordering only sometimes needs to be exercised with militarized border controls. In most cities, the market can accomplish it just fine, a set of ordering mechanisms that leaves people suspicious that their exclusions are somehow their own fault, that they are confined to the outside because of some personal, familial or cultural inadequacies.

It is easy enough to get to Vancouver from Surrey any time. The train gets you downtown to downtown in forty minutes. It's no real hassle to go shopping, eat dinner, or even find a place to live. There are no rules that prohibit someone from Surrey renting or buying a place in the city, and of course many people make that move. But as one of my colleagues says, "Vancouver is kind of a place for white or Asian people who have their shit together." He is not ruling out moving there necessarily, but as someone who claims he is none of those things (the last is debatable), he is functionally ruling it out. He knows Vancouver is there, but also knows what it would take to relocate and what it would cost him.

Sub-urbs or banlieues or shantytowns or favelas are not camps in the literal sense—and they are certainly not prisons—but thinking about Mbembe's work is to ask after states of exception and their myriad forms. Words that social theorists use, like *abandonment*, *expulsion*, *displacement* and the many other terms to describe getting kicked out, evicted, asked to leave, or never invited, all make sense, but it also feels shitty to be described as helpless, as these descriptors suggest.

Sometimes being in Surrey feels like an exclusion for sure, like it is outside the city, but mostly not, mostly it feels like being *inside* something. It also feels like there is a parallel urban world, one that connects various scattered sub-urbs via material and cultural grooves. In the same ways that money and people and relationships flow from certain global cities to other global cities, sub-urbs are also connected to each other, a flow of people and ideas and goods that operates almost entirely outside the field of dominant urban visions.

4

In wandering to other cities, I am not looking for evidentiary "proof" or disproofs of my analyses. Nor is my goal here to produce a taxonomy of sub-urbanization, but I am curious if my experiences in Surrey or any other sub-urb is specific, or generalizable at all, and whether any of that travels out of North America. So I went to Rabat, Morocco. I am embarrassingly unilingual and was looking for something to shake my parochial torpor, so I signed myself up for a month of full-time language classes in Rabat: French in the morning, Arabic in the afternoon.

For a middle-aged white guy from Canada, Rabat is a pretty easy entrée into Morocco. I arrived in Casablanca looking and feeling like a pile of dirty laundry and was charitably picked up at the airport and driven the hour and a half north to my hosts. I stayed in Rabat with a sweet family in a comfortable room overlooking a central intersection, a five-minute walk from the language school. After a couple of weeks, my own family came to join me, and we moved into an apartment in a swanky neighborhood a short tram ride away.

Rabat is not a tourist destination and has a boring reputation, especially compared with other frenetic Moroccan cities. It is the capital and seat of government, so bureaucratic sensibilities spill easily over into everyday life. Places like Marrakech and Fez are humming hives of frantic touristic hustle, Casablanca is the thudding center of capital, coastal towns like Agadir rock a chill beach vibe, but Rabat is the dull city where most visitors pass through quickly en route to somewhere sexier.

But it's still a Moroccan city, which means it has plenty of flavor, and is most certainly way the hell funkier than Vancouver (which is admittedly not hard to be). It has all the predictably palimpsestic urban development of a city that has history dating at least to Phoenicians, but is navigably sized and comprehensible, with an excellent streetcar system that criss-crosses the city and relatively tame street and traffic flows. The whole place has an easy rhythm that I quickly got in step with. For a visitor, especially a North American one, the claustrophobic commercial hustle and mercantile bustle of Moroccan street life takes a beat to get used to, but, mostly owing to the kindnesses of my hosts, I settled in pretty smoothly. There are some touristy things to do in Rabat, but not really. Mainly, it's just an administrative capital going about its business.

I was sitting in classes most every day. But when I wandered, it was quickly clear that some well-trod processes of aspirational global-city restructuring are very much in play. Governmental, military and royal apparatuses take up most of the built life of the city, but new capital forays are rebuilding train stations into colossuses, there are major shopping mall and office developments in the wealthier areas, and of course, heavy doses of upmarket housing, condos and hotels are being eagerly administered in aspirational neighborhoods.

For all its Maghrebian novelty (novel to me, anyway), Rabat felt comfortably familiar in many ways, which I partly attribute to seeing commonplace kinds of displacements and dispossessions happening all around. That's weird to say, but it's true. There was something absurdly comforting in hearing my college-aged language instructors talking among themselves, complaining about rent increases and condos, using the English word *gentrification* in both French and Arab conversations, in *exactly* the same tones that I hear my own kids use when they are with their pals, with *just* the same sneers capturing that combo of righteousness, dismay, resignation and snark.

5

Rabat is about the same size as Vancouver, with a population of around six hundred thousand, and is bordered to the north by the Bou Regreg river, with the city of Salé on the other side. Salé is older, and has a significantly bigger population than Rabat, but is often described as a "commuter city," or the poorer, homelier, working-class residential complement to Rabat—which reminded me in so many ways of the relationship between Surrey and Vancouver, or Gresham and Portland, or so many other cities.

Salé and Rabat are properly understood as one city: an urban region or metro area with segregated components, part of the Rabat–Salé–Kenitra municipal region that is stitched together with an excellent train-tram system, and as far as I could tell, people moved pretty seamlessly up and down the coast between the three cities on a daily basis.

After a few weeks, I began to have a passable navigational sense of the city's geography and physical structure. It became easy to move between neighborhoods, but that ease was tempered by my poor understanding of basic Moroccan social and political milieus. Rabat is a postcolonial city, gaining independence in 1955, and Morocco is a "unitary semi-constitutional monarchy." This means that there is a democratic governmental structure that carries out legislative, juridical and administrative operations, but Morocco's king has ultimate control, veto power and massive influence on everything, most critically, overseeing the military and foreign affairs. It became increasingly evident to me that I had never really spent much (any?) time in an actual kingdom before, and I was pretty ignorant about what that meant for urban development.

Morocco's history is a bewilderingly dense set of overlapping influences and periods of occupation from early Phoenician, Carthaginian and Roman settlements, to long successions of Berber, Alawite and Arab dynasties, to Barbary Corsair pirates who controlled Salé and Rabat as a republic in the 1600s, to Portuguese and Ottoman incursions, to periods when France and Spain carved out "zones of influence" as colonial protectorates. But what I am most interested in here is Morocco's recent experience with the rapid movement from French and Spanish colonial occupation to independence (including significant US military support for "liberation") and its transition to a densely hybrid governance model.

Each of these shifts in sovereignty and control has come with heavy doses of displacement, expulsions and violence, and Morocco's frothy and still emergent forms of power and government are fertile ground to ask: Are the new forms of peripheralization that are so evident across the country, and certainly in Rabat, something new? Or is this just the same-old, same-old story of power pushing around poor people, just with new names and different branding?

The best-known analysis of Rabat is still Janet Abu-Lughod's 1981 classic *Rabat: Urban Apartheid in Morocco*—which appeared just a decade after her equally influential book *Cairo* (1971) —and in many ways her work still sets the table for subsequent city research in North Africa. Abu-Lughod's study of Rabat–Salé closely analyzed census data from a decade earlier and argued that the city could only be understood in terms of *segregation*—a colonial logic first inscribed by the French that assiduously separated Europeans from Moroccans, creating and recreating "caste cleavages" that were enforced spatially, culturally and economically. She argued that through the 1900s, that system slowly morphed into new forms of segregation that were deployed along deeply etched class and ethnic lines that defined residential and commercial limits to development. So, while Rabat was once a "caste city," it became a "class city." But caste (which, in her loose usage, roughly connotes to "status") was so deeply ingrained that the structure of the city remained "caste-like," resembling a form of apartheid that grooved lines of residential and commercial possibilities, which held even through ongoing massive rural–urban population influxes and shifts of power.

Abu-Lughod's analysis neatly frames one of the central questions in this book, maybe *the* central question: Is this new phenomenon of displacements that are expelling poor people from the centers of cities across the world something new? Or is what we are witnessing just another iteration of the same techniques and technologies of power that have always displaced and dispossessed people? I am of course most interested in this analysis, hoping that understanding these expulsions might give us better ideas on how to resist. Can the responses and resistances in Rabat teach us anything here in Surrey? Does Rabat reveal anything particular about new and future urban forms, here and afar?

Helpfully, Abu-Lughod spoke directly to those questions in a terrific 2007 paper titled "The Challenge of Comparative Case Studies," in which she addressed Loïc Wacquant's work comparing "hyperghettos" in Chicago with banlieues in Paris. More on that in a minute, but first I want to ask if the example of Rabat reveals something specific about multiple overlapping forms of power and control—colonial, royal, tribal, piratic, neoliberal and so on—the kinds of bewilderingly shifting and overlapping sovereignties that are so readily apparent in so many peripheral urban zones.

The fulcrum for understanding Rabat's modern history is the omnipresence of colonial rationalities: everything about Rabat through the past hundred years is inflected by French fears and hungers. Right from their arrival, French officials were terrified of racial mixing, and deeply suspicious of urban density as a petri dish for revolt. At the same time, colonial officials were constantly maneuvering to thwart traditional tribal, Berber and rival European powers from gaining traction. In 1912 the French moved the capital city from Fez—in the heart of a particularly hostile anti-colonial region—to Rabat, where they could establish a Casablanca–Rabat–Kenitra economic corridor to exploit the rich agricultural and mineral wealth of the coastal plains and easily siphon resources to the metropole.

Salé, which had long been the dominant economic power on the Bou Regreg, was in steep decline as piracy was collapsing, so it was relegated to supporting Rabat through commuter, industrial and port functions. French officials' twin obsessions of discouraging urban concentration while ensuring racialized segregations found expression in robustly energetic agricultural policies, which heavily subsidized food production, keeping native Moroccans occupied working the land, while cities remained relatively decongested. When surplus rural populations did migrate to Rabat, often evicted by land-grabbing French estates, they were pushed to Salé, where unplanned slums—*bidonvilles*—began to appear by the middle of the 1900s and remain all across the metro region.

I had researched several of these areas before I arrived in Rabat, so a couple of times a week I got Karim, one of my host family's cousins, to give me a ride out to the sub-urbs. I had some ideas about where I wanted to go and had read about several cool social and housing projects underway in Karyane El Oued and Oued Akreuch. But honestly, I am still not 100 percent certain I ever got where I was aiming. Karim was a good guy, and we sure laughed a lot together—but between me wantonly butchering the French and Arabic languages and his singular focus on interrogating me about the NBA, Megan Thee Stallion, and American life in general—we got lost repeatedly. We mostly ended up drinking coffee, smoking shisha and talking shit with a bunch of his buddies, somewhere way out on the edges of Salé, which to me counted as quality research.

6

Everywhere we went on the outskirts of Rabat and Salé, I kept looking for coherence in the urban form: some kind of obvious slums or informal settlements, or villages that had been subsumed by sprawl, or middle-class enclaves, or rich-people gated enclaves. I kept seeing all of these communities, but kind of jumbled together. As soon as I was in one area that started to make some sense to me, it would shift abruptly, throwing me off. I was trying to find a genealogy of the city's peripheral growth, but any plausible narratives alluded me.

To try and make sense of it, I leaned heavily on Max Rousseau and Maryame Amarouche, two very active urban scholars living in Rabat.[12] When I went to Max's family's place, he explained the history and development of his neighborhood, and made it very clear to me how central the deeply entwined royal and military prerogatives are to understanding the city's patterns of settlement and displacement. Property allocation has always been a critical tool for maintaining the crown's control, and parcels of land and housing are often allocated in ways that are both more brutal and more subtle than simple market forces. It is very clear that patterns of peripheralized displacement are unfolding in Rabat, but I was not exactly sure how to approach it.

One night when we were out with a couple of pals in Casablanca, I was telling the table about this book project exploring urban peripheralization, and one person paused for a beat and then said, "Of course poor people don't live in downtown Casablanca now. It's all tourists and wealthy apartments." The response was delivered in an immediate and off-the-cuff manner, one that suggested I was being either a little simple or condescending in my presentation. I was intrigued, obviously, because it seemed to substantiate so much of the theorizing I had arrived at in studying Surrey–Portland–Ferguson and sub-urbs across the globe, but I cautioned myself (again) against any facile, if appealing, universalizing leaps.

When I got back to Rabat, I tried a different approach by asking Maryame and Max if Rabat had a downtown, or central district. The medina is the city's historical center of commerce, but I was struggling to find something that I recognized as a "downtown." I was staying across the street from the main train station, and that felt pretty central, but is that a center? Is the palace rightfully thought of as the center of the city? Is that even the right way to start thinking about Rabat? Max sniffed me out right away:

> That's a complex question. It depends on what is meant by "center." Centrality is defined as opposed to a periphery, but these notions are dynamic and evolving. They are also subjective: an individual or a group can claim to be located in the center while others will object that it actually belongs to the periphery . . .
>
> If we take the view of the dominant, which is usually the one that ends up imposing the definition of the center (the "center" and the "periphery" of the "space conceived" by the bureaucracy and the bourgeoisie, according to Lefebvre), then we realize that the center of Rabat-Salé has moved over the course of history. This is not surprising: the agglomeration is home to the capital of Morocco. It is therefore closely linked to the changes in the political economy of Morocco, marked in the twentieth century by the turmoil of colonization, then independence.

This was a super-sharp comment that immediately grounded my thinking about Rabat and Salé in a different way. For almost all its history, Morocco has been subject to imperial ambitions, but it was one of the very last countries in the "Scramble for Africa" to be fully colonized by a European power.

The French were not able to colonize Morocco using the same methods they deployed in other parts of the Maghreb. In Algeria, for example, the French occupiers destroyed old medinas and built entirely new cities, while in Morocco they attempted a different set of strategies based on containment and segregation. The Moroccan model enclosed native Moroccans in the extant central city medinas, and then enacted strong agricultural policies to discourage rural-to-urban migration. This left the bulk of cities, including almost all of Rabat, available for French planners to build and rebuild urban neighborhoods based on elegant and airy design and contemporary, European, City Beautiful–esque planning principles. This created a very different colonial urbanist point of departure, involuted in some ways from other colonized African cities.

Under French rule, urban planning was under military control—generals who were also urban planners, and who were fluent in very specific exclusionary tactics and strategies. The French planners were able to create proto-zoning techniques with extremely strong barriers, to keep races separated, and to maintain urban control. Post-independence, these same strategies were carried on by the monarchy—described by nationalist leader Mehdi Ben Barka as a new form of internalized colonialism—that saw the French retain control over the country via Moroccan bourgeoisie who continued to closely align themselves with their former rulers.

This core rural–urban strategy—strong agricultural policies supported with huge subsidies to keep people out of cities where factories and students could foment revolution—lasted until the mid-1970s. Amid global oil-debt crises, the United States and the IMF arrived in Morocco in force, bringing with them neoliberal structural readjustments, market liberalization reforms, "modernizations" of regulatory environments, new financialized mechanisms, and all the rest of the accoutrements of a swift and volatile shift to a private market–driven economy.

These reforms could not abide by the massive subsidization of the Moroccan agricultural and food sectors, so in short order the country's priorities were transformed, throwing huge numbers of people into poverty and food insecurity, leading to rural exodus, huge influxes into cities and bread riots. This new instability reinforced the Kingdom's commitment to militaristic urban planning designed to separate races, classes and castes.

As Maryame explained, one of the most obvious and effective of these tools in Rabat is the creation of the Green Belt, which hems in the city from the south:

> It is really important to understand the urban tool of the Green Belt. I have studied this Green Belt closely and interviewed many people. It is not just a planning or social good; much more than that, it is a securitization tool. The Belt is very strategically located between Rabat and Temara (a peripheral community where many rural arrivals land), and while at first glance it is a very nice place with an urban forest and lots of places to walk and play, you can't penetrate or cross it easily—there are armed guard towers all through the forest.
>
> And this helps to understand Rabat. It is the global market that shapes the city, yes, but in the context of an authoritarian state. Rabat is the capital; it is bizarrely clean, with police everywhere. The castle sits ostentatiously in the middle of the city, administratively dominating the culture.
>
> Rabat is very contained physically—by the Atlantic Ocean on one side, the Bou Regreg Valley in the north and east, then closed in by the Green Belt on the southern side.
>
> These physical elements are part of the tools the state uses to control and manage Rabat.

Maryame emphasized that it is useful to compare peripheralization in Rabat to patterns in the Global North, but there are critical specificities in Global South cities, in Morocco and Rabat particularly. "Peripheralization is happening because people get pushed from the city center. I am working in many municipalities around Rabat, but I think the difference is in Moroccan cities—and cities in the Global South—we have different ways of building."

She described the informal settlements around Rabat where poor people, particularly families arriving from agricultural areas, build their own houses and neighborhoods. These places are not "informal" settlements—a false designation constructed by planning regimes—but well-built communities. Maryame explained:

The authorities create all these rules for houses that people cannot afford to live up to. They are healthy, organized and safe homes; they are traditionally built. But because planners want to produce the city with adherence to French traditions, they produce "informal settlements" that are only made informal because of rules.

7

This explains some of my inability to discern coherence on the peripheries of Rabat. The constraint on the central city by una- pologetic royal, military and administrative power is clear and unmistakable, but to understand the gentrification of the newly attractive urban cores and resulting displacement to the edges of the city, any analysis has to focus on the specificities of the local context. Morocco's special brew of colonial, authoritarian and market forces compel and construct very curious kinds of peripheries.

French planners' obsession with segregation meant that between the old central medinas and the agricultural lands where Moroccans were contained, colonial settlers could sprawl all across the fertile peripheries of the city, building huge villas, farms and estates, punctuated with wide leafy promenades, plenty of parklands, vineyards and walled communities. After independ- ence and the colonial administrative exoduses, Moroccan and French bourgeoise took over much of this land, but with the shift to neoliberal regimes, driven home by the end of GATT (General Agreement on Tariffs and Trade) and the impositions of the World Trade Organization (consecrated in 1994 with the Marrakesh Agreement), Moroccan agricultural markets collapsed, and all this sprawling land became far less attractive.

Local (and foreign) capitalists were stuck with money to invest but without agricultural exports to profit from, so they needed to put it somewhere else. In an era of neoliberal capital mobility, their hungry eyes soon turned to the city center. The new inner- city property market had to be revitalized and its lower-income residents moved out, just like in so many cities across the globe. But in Rabat, as populations have moved further out, they have encountered multiple tidal forces: rural residents washing into the city, extant wealthier enclaves whose residents maintain their estates and villas, and the eddies and pools of settlements that are created by securitized and physical borders.

This creates a bewildering mix all through Rabat's urban periphery, consisting of "informal" bidonvilles, walled communities, stable-but-poor planned communities, middle-class neighborhoods, newer bourgeois property enclaves, older and modest farms—all jumbled together, and existing cheek by jowl. Thrown into this pot are semi-functional "satellite cities" that were built as new housing for poor and middle-class residents that have failed to coalesce.

In the early years of the twenty-first century, the Moroccan state sold huge swaths of land around Rabat to French, Malaysian, Middle Eastern and local investors to build "new cities" to (re)house residents being expelled from newly unaffordable neighborhoods. Huge numbers of people moved to these areas, but the 2008 financial crisis put an end to investment, developers escaped with their money, construction halted and now across the Rabat periphery lies an urban archipelago: sizable communities of people stuck, with decent houses they have paid for, but marooned, with no transit or jobs anywhere nearby.

This jumble reminds me of sub-urbs all over the world. It's a spatial and a social form I've been trying to name when I describe Surrey. The desperate grasping for any kind of investment on Vancouver's periphery leaves the civic infrastructure bereft of sufficiently organized regulatory capacity, creating a seemingly out-of-control, unplanned milieu. Surrey is a mess in both the awesome and ugly senses for all kinds of people with all kinds of agendas, including the one of simply securing cheaper housing.

This gets us back to the question of a "center" in Rabat. Is there one? And why we should care about trying to identify one there or anywhere? What is to be gained by naming *this* the center and *that* the periphery?

Janet Abu-Lughod harbored hopes that the deep colonial attachment to the segregation she had documented would weaken after independence, but that optimism quickly faded. After the departure of the French, the wealthiest Moroccans, the ones closest to the Royal Palace, settled in the new city, where they benefit from an omnipresent police presence, globalized commercial offerings and elite schools. Because of its geographical centrality, the old medina has maintained its market function for the working classes, but it is newly vulnerable to commercial gentrification built around international tourism.

Given that Rabat's medina has recently been classified as a UNESCO heritage site, it is likely that a modest uptick in tourism will cleanse both the medina and kasbah of working-class shops and residents. Maryame makes the argument that although the influence of global capital, tourism and foreign investment has been heavily documented and theorized, the impacts of Moroccans living abroad, especially in Europe, cannot be underestimated. Fueled by their desire to both invest in their home country and realize strong returns, a huge amount of investment is returning to the country and Rabat via remittances, land purchases and the development of second homes. The exact scale of investment is hard to track, but its influence glaring, and it is especially visible in the medina and older neighborhoods that have a nostalgic resonance.

In some sense, the medina does cling to a form of centrality— for tourists, remittance investments and lower-end commercial activity—but really, the modern center has long since moved. In the 1980s, King Hassan II built a new district, adjacent to the Royal Palace: Hay Riad. The district was designed on lands historically allocated by the sultan to a particular tribe charged with defending the gates of the city. The military function of the tribe has become obsolete since the creation of a modern army, so the land has changed its use to become the site of a hyper-modern district with luxury villas and buildings and the head offices of many ministries and large firms, augmented by ultra-modern shopping centers and supermarkets.

The creation of Hay Riad has fulfilled both a political and economic logic: political, because it is about "loyalty" to the monarchy's senior officials (military command, police and administrative) who have purchased Hay Riad at prices well below the market; and economic, because the district was conceived from the outset as the signal of a country open to globalization, or more specifically to outside investment. Hay Riad is the new "center" designed by the government in Rabat. With its ultra-modern architecture, its accessibility, and its concentration of commercial, economic, political, administrative and residential functions, it is what comes closest to an American downtown today.

It is easy to make an argument that Hay Riad is now "the" center of Rabat, but as is the case everywhere else, the claim that there can ever be *one* center reveals and obscures with the same breath. As usual, trying to identify a single center is just another exercise of power.

8

Shortly after leaving Morocco, I became really curious about whether my thinking about centers and peripheries makes any sense in a really giant megalopolis. Rabat, Portland, St. Louis and Vancouver are all similar-sized cities and metro regions, but London is just a whole other thing altogether. It's a city with a massive population for sure, but also so iconic and exists as such a heavy global fulcrum: it is the center of empire, the aggregator of unthinkable amounts of wealth—some earned, but mostly stolen. It is the touchstone for centuries of urban imaginaries, a distribution center for intellectual, cultural and social capitals, *the* self-styled "city on a hill," standing above all the rest.

The day after I arrived in London, I accidentally found myself in the middle of a massive Brexit rally—this one very aggressively pro-Leave. I followed for a bit, and it was everything you might imagine: wave after wave of old people waving Union Jacks, screaming football yobs, clusters of middle-aged moms, a few obvious fascist types, and a lot of high-energy nationalist chants rhyming awkwardly with "Leave." It wasn't a riot, but it sure felt like it could become one.

London was (and is) always very heavily pro-Remain, so I had no idea where all these people came from, but there sure were a ton of them. One of the very many fractures Brexit conversations revealed or exacerbated, both in the lead-up and in the ongoing reverberations that have followed, is the tremendous divide between London and other British towns and cities. I am not sure how many of the people at that event lived in London, but my wholly uninformed first guess was not that many.

Veteran TV announcer Jon Snow was there too, reporting live from Parliament Square:

Police are now wearing riot gear. Police dogs are patrolling. The mood has changed. We cannot confirm whether any arrests have been made . . . It has been the most extraordinary day. A day which has seen . . . I've never seen so many white people in one place . . . It's an extraordinary story—there are people everywhere, there are crowds everywhere.

Channel 4 had to apologize publicly for these comments—the "white people" bit in particular. Snow was later cleared of any wrongdoing, but he was publicly cautioned to stop intimating that Brexit and white supremacy had anything to do with one another.

Brexit has since become a very murky story, with many more chapters unfolding since the day of that protest, and many more still to come. But as I watched that rally, it struck me that there are a number of common themes animating all that anger and frustration. Among them are a bedrock belief in Anglo excep-tionalism, a resentment of immigrants and their penetration into British society, and a loosely defined nostalgia for a now-lost halcyon golden era, made that much more painful by deindustri-alization and the resulting deep pockets of poverty and precarity.

Brexit—both before and since—has been tiresomely dissected from every possible direction, but it is commonly understood as the kind of eruptive convulsion that marks the decline of empires. All that nostalgia unapologetically references the salad days of English dominance—a wistfulness for a time when it was literally true that the sun never set on the British Empire. Brexit is a whole lot more complex than just that empiric nostalgia alone, but that history is entangled with every Leave argument.

Britain did not invent colonialism, but it near perfected it. Have you ever seen a map of all the countries Great Britain has *not* invaded? There are only twenty-two that have thus far avoided its hungry gaze, scattered across the map seemingly randomly—Uzbekistan, Bolivia, Ivory Coast and Sweden, to name a few. Colonialism resides at the heart of Britishness—a core faith that Britain sits at the center of the world and all the rest is a periphery, a periphery that should be grateful to feed the "commonwealth" with bodies, resources and land.

A quick spin through any of the spectacular museums in London bulwarks this notion with some force: the rugs and bones and clothes and tools and valuables of people from every corner of the world are gathered there for catalogued and measured consumption. Museums mostly seem like barbaric institutions to me, but the same logic is repeated over and over, as a way of being in the world: coldly pillaging the periphery to feed a voraciously accumulating center.

This British form of domination was exported as a political apparatus to the colonies. Canada, like so many others, was founded and designed as a pantry of raw materials to feed the empiric British center. But the logic was also replicated internally within Canada, as the nation's founding documents laid plain that the peripheral provinces were forged as natural resource collection zones to support "central" Canada.

The centre-plus-periphery political construction is a pervasively common one, and is among the foundations of British political sensibilities. But is that a way to make some sense of London, or is it just too fractured and ungainly a city for that kind of analysis? Is London even really a "city" in the everyday sense?

Making spatial sense of London, even just in its basic outlines, takes some work and linguistic contortion. There is something of a ring road, or the "Orbital Motorway"—the inner ring of which is called the North and South Circular Roads; the outer ring, the M25—that encircles what is called "Greater London." If you put a pin in the geographic center of Greater London, you get the "City of London," which comprises what was the historic city and is now occasionally referred to as the Central Business District (CBD). When the "City" is capitalized, it refers to a tiny district that is engulfed physically by the actual city, the metropolitan London. The City has spilled over its original cartographic constraints but remains a separate enclave with its own governing administration, and remains one of, if not *the*, primary gathering point in the world for transnational capital. The firms and organizations conglomerated in the City coordinate and control vast and disparate reserves of extractive wealth, with tentacles reaching to every corner of the global economy. Does that make the City the center of the city? In some senses, sure.

But there is also such a dizzying array of administrative and governing bodies in metropolitan London, overlapping and criss-crossing, piled up and bumping into one another, that "London" is defined in all kinds of ways, official and unofficial, for all kinds of purposes. In many cities, there are at least physically obvious "downtowns" to aim for, but that's tricky to do in London, or even get a bead on where the boundaries of any London might be drawn.

In addition to the City of London, there is also the City of Westminster, one of several Inner London boroughs, that also holds its own city status, and geographically resides right in the middle of Greater London. Westminster contains many of the iconic spots that tourists or observers might think of as central to the city: the Houses of Parliament, 10 Downing Street, Oxford Street, Piccadilly, Soho. Even more than that, it is the site of St. James's and Buckingham Palaces, the heart of the monarchy, the seat of empire. So surely that's the center of London.

But then, maybe not. Westminster is the center of national government, but London's City Hall, the functional administrative center of the city, is nowhere close. Once five kilometers away, across the river from the City, City Hall has now moved even further east. Maybe it is more realistic to look to Canary Wharf on the Isle of Dogs—a tight concentration of glistening spikes that looks much more like a modern downtown, and houses so much capital clout it makes your head spin.

9

London helps disorient my reflexive approaches to seeing a city, in part because it is so confounding to choose a center there—it is functionally not viable to even speak of London as an entity, as a discrete thing. So then what? I know the place a little, but not nearly well enough, so I asked Loretta Lees to help me see the city. Loretta lived and/or worked in London for over two decades and is an internationally renowned scholar of global urbanism, urban policy, architecture and public space. She's best known though for her long-term work on gentrification and has played a central role in debates around what she now calls "planetary gentrification."

Loretta's also a really nice and down-to-earth person, someone who you like within about twenty seconds of meeting. She is a warm presence and generous in sharing her easy grasp of critical social theory. She often speaks of her working-class family and you can see that sensibility surfacing often in her observations and analyses. Loretta also knows Vancouver well, having done a postdoc here in the '90s, so she was an ideal person to help me figure out how to approach London.

I was staying with my pal Sam up in Hampstead, so Loretta and I met over in the Heath one afternoon and spent a long afternoon wandering around, talking about London, taking in the views from various hilly vantage points. Over the course of subsequent emails and phone and video calls with her, it became ever more evident to me how difficult, maybe impossible, it is to easily compare London to other cities. It is just a whole other thing in so many ways, and peripheralizations take on whole other shades and trajectories.

For starters, just the enormity of London presents all kinds of conceptual challenges for urban thinking. The suburbanization of poverty was not invented in Europe—Britain has always pushed its poor out of desirable central districts—but the suburbs, especially in London, have a distinct spatial, social and structural character. That's maybe the first thing to note: just how urban so many so-called suburbs, especially the inner burbs, feel there. You can go a long way out from the CBD and drop into places that feel like wholly separate cities but are popularly understood as London "suburbs." With multiple commercial high streets, substantial foot traffic, and essentially similar levels of residential and commercial density as anywhere near the river (many have their own "town centers," in planning parlance), these are suburbs, but they don't look much like their North American, or European, cousins.

More than that, suburbs in London tend to be more multi-ethnic. So many sub-urbs across North America and Europe are highly racialized, but also highly segregated. London suburbs tend to reflect sub-urban racialized banishments to varying degrees, but have a far more mixed character, both in terms of race and class, than I am familiar with. A huge amount of that, as Loretta wanted me to understand, owes to the Tube.

It is hard to underestimate the ongoing and historical impact of the London Underground. Right from its founding in 1863, the Tube nurtured previously unthinkable dreams and gave shape and form to the city, creating new elasticities and unlocking dormant capital. The Victorian city was engulfed by industrial transformation, shimmering with new wealth but also wracked by pollution and overcrowding, brutal housing and manufactured poverty. In response, the cross-class aspirational dream of a detached house, clean air, healthy water and a back garden reverberated through Victorian urban imaginaries and literatures, a yearning for flight from unsanitary urban wretchedness.

The Underground made escape plausible, enthusiastically stretching distances between home and job, intimately linking previously disconnected places. The dream of a "good, healthy family home" all of a sudden became possible for masses of people. It also gave wings to the dreams of capital, releasing the value of distant land parcels with startling efficiency—all made possible by the reach of the Tube. The multiple early owners of various lines were hardly ignorant of the possibilities and duly noted that the further their tracks reached, the more people were served; the more they could charge for tickets; and the greater the freight carriage possibilities.

What is more, as lines extended, line owners purchased land, not just to accommodate the rail infrastructure, but also for housing developments, especially around stations. It became a happy little circle of capital—riders, the traffic of goods, and land sales all supporting and spurring one another—with train cars covered in advertising literature for new developments, stations built as transport nodes, and each new estate feeding in new passengers that paid for new extensions. This constant growth and extension meant that by 2011, 55 percent of the total population of England and Wales lived in suburbs, which are now home to 73 percent of all British immigrants. It is also possible to claim that half of Londoners live in the suburbs, although, without a common definition of what suburbs are and what they are not, that claim is both intriguing and functionally useless.[13]

10

I was curious to see what some of these transit-oriented suburban communities looked and felt like, so I set out very early one spring day and walked north across the Heath and up to Hampstead Garden Suburb. I knew in advance that it really isn't "transit oriented" nor the kind of community I am most interested in, but it has "suburb" right there in its name. Plus it was close, so I figured what the hell.

Despite the name, Hampstead Garden Suburb does not adhere much to Ebenezer Howard's classic Garden City principles, and it required a special Act of Parliament in 1906 to circumvent extant bylaws and building codes. The creation of HGS is important in some ways because it harbinged post–World War II suburban spatial ethics: the Hampstead Garden Suburb Act delineates for communities a very low housing density, wide, tree-lined roads, houses that are separated by hedges not walls(!), and a vigilantly maintained, quiet atmosphere.

In its founding documents, HGS was required to be a mixed-income development, and at one point in its history it had a reputation for harboring liberal intellectual and artistic types, but those days appear long past. If you breathe deeply while wandering along its broad, tranquil streets, you can feel the restrained bougieness filling your lungs. There is no industry nearby, just the occasional twee little shop, a couple of highly rated schools with wildly posh visages, many tennis courts visible from the street, and extremely well-maintained public and private greenery. In some ways the HGS is a suburban ideal: residential, exclusive, contained, constrained, and very controlled. But in many other ways it's just another snobby upper-middle-class enclave inside the city limits.

Realizing I'd made a misstep in my planning, and suddenly feeling intrusive, I beat a quick exit. As I did, I remembered reading a story about how the residents' association had implemented a series of rules issuing red and yellow cards to anyone caught using noisy devices like lawn mowers. I kept my head down and tried not to let my boots smack the pavement too loudly. The whole experience was useful to remember the surprisingly pervasive and resilient garden-city influences on British urban planning, but this was clearly not what I was looking for.

I headed for the Tube and consulted a list of sites to visit I had made over the past couple of days. I'd been at a few events that week and had asked people where modestly incomed folks were getting pushed to, where everyday people were moving. I then pared that list down, settling on a few places that several people mentioned, and set a route. I spent the rest of that Tuesday on trains, heading out on one line, getting off to snack and wander around in each place for an hour or so, then hopping back on and rebounding the other way. Over the course of a long day, I hit Wembley, Tooting, Barking and Woodford, all neighborhoods that might qualify as "peripheral."

All four places are well within the limits of the M25 and thus part of Greater London, and all take forty minutes to one hour to get to via the Tube (heading in different directions on different lines), measured from King's Cross or Oxford Circus. All are highly diverse areas; some describe themselves as independent towns, or administrative centers of separate boroughs (just to add to the wild mélange of London governance structures), and all sort of reminded me of Surrey, at least if I squinted just right.

Then again, they didn't remind me of Surrey at all. All of these places can trace their built histories back hundreds and hundreds of years, their recorded histories much further; even their "contemporary" forays as commuter neighborhoods within London took place in the last half of the 1800s. It seems a stretch to compare these places, with their old stone churches and rowhouses and their long relationships with the rest of London, to fledgling suburbs of North America, nor to anywhere in the Global South.

I spent a chunk of time the night before my field trip day perusing Craigslist ads for apartments, and there were lots of offerings that struck me as relatively affordable, but also a significant number that seemed wickedly expensive. As I toured around each area, I made sure to drop by a few of those addresses and had some of my suspicions confirmed. I heard all four of these areas described as "a bit far out there," and while many of the housing ads took pains to assure prospective renters that the commute wasn't *that* bad, it was clear that the higher-priced flats were always within close walking distance of a station. The rentals that were cheaper were on noisier high streets, in obviously shitty buildings, or a good ways off from a station.

It was obvious that each of the four areas I visited was in some stage of substantial transition: each had the predictable swanky developments popping up and promotional reaches seeking to attract upscale residents, and it wasn't hard to find evidence of good ole class struggle. All these neighborhoods have had recent anti-gentrification flare-ups and protests, and echoes of displacement or the threat of it were everywhere. You know this feeling—it's almost a smell in the air, or a visceral tingle as a neighborhood is bracing itself. I suspect that real estate agents are trained to identify these sensations, like a truffle pig snuffling around, hunting for rent gaps.

As I was scarfing down breakfast at a tiny café in an indoor market in Tooting, the friendly, stout guy named Amir who owned the place came and sat with me. I think he was a little concerned with the speed with which I put back the pretty significant pile of food, which seemed to exacerbate a twitch he had of touching his left ear with his left hand repeatedly. He asked what I was doing in Tooting, then chuckled and said I was at least five years too late, that all the cheap rent had moved from Brixton to Clapham to here, but now even Tooting was pricey. He said it was just the way things went, and that now the neighborhood was well known as one of the "coolest neighborhoods in the world" and that was that. Tooting is definitely a great spot, but I silently scoffed when he said that, but turns out he could back up this "coolest" claim.[14] He explained it all started with London's hosting of the 2012 Summer Olympics, as people were "running away" from all the inner-city investment. He also said, with a smile and a wink, that business was better than it had ever been.

11

There are few cities in the world that are as defined and disfigured by global-city processes as London: one of the (maybe *the*) premier landing spots for global capital, it features a hyper-dense concentration of high-end financialized industries, which in turn are a magnet for more of the same. These industries—in banking, insurance, finance, real estate, venture capital especially—in turn nurture a thick ecosystem of "creative class" types fluent in marketing, advertising, design and technology.

As in every other city that the Olympics have blighted, and as Amir noted to me, the 2012 London games enthusiastically accelerated these processes, with an unprecedented concentration of creative-class professionals aggregating in inner-city neighborhoods, where walkable high streets, good flat whites, bike lanes and smartly themed bars are in strong supply. As Richard Florida, the omnipresent proselytizing shepherd of bourgeois urban restructuring, noted as far back as 2013:

> London's creative class totals 1.7 million workers, comprising 41.6 percent of its workforce . . .
>
> London's creative class is highly concentrated in and around the city center. The darkest areas of purple [Florida is referring here to a London map coded by economic class], where the creative class makes up roughly 80 percent of residents, are in and around the core, including Kensington, Chelsea, the City of London and Camden . . . The areas of highest creative class concentration (the darkest purple areas on the map) radiate north and west from the center . . .
>
> The service class, the red areas on the map, is pushed out to the city's periphery, and is arrayed in three large areas to the

northwest, northeast and south of the city. The service class is London's largest class, numbering 1.9 million residents and comprising 46.5 percent of the city's workforce. The service class is also highly concentrated and clustered.[15]

Florida went on to note that he saw no neighborhoods where working-class residents comprised the majority, and, in his reckoning, the working class make up only 11.6 percent of all employed people in London.

All these designations are of course contestable and performative: the math behind that last number, for example, really depends on how you define "working class," which is of course a sketchy act of taxonomy, and he was just flat wrong about "service-class" residents living solely on the periphery—it's a demonstrable fact that they lived in council estates all over London at the time of his observation, and many remain there today. But I think his general point holds, and the demographic map he points to matches what I have seen in London, and most everywhere else too. Those patterns of displacement are super familiar. Is it just that in London the processes of peripheralization, like most everything else in the city, are a little more complex, a little more capitalized, a little faster?

But it's not all that simple, as Loretta kept explaining to me. It is an easy mistake to fit London into a common pattern of expulsions, to see capital spreading out like an infection from the City, to impose an inversion narrative, but, as like everywhere, London has its own nuanced story. Residing at the heart of this book is a certain kind of comparative urbanism, or maybe better, a syncretic urbanism, an attempt to understand a little about London to help make sense of what's in front of us everywhere else. And because London is so Global North–iconic—it's literally where Ruth Glass birthed the term "gentrification" in 1964—it is tempting to view it as an exemplar that other cities reflexively mimic.

Fortunately, Loretta has done considerable thinking about how theory travels. She has written as much as anybody about gentrification and while she is highly sensitive to the problems with uncritically deploying it as a term, she still sees significant value in understanding London and cities across the globe through that lens. One of the key difficulties, however, in universally applying *gentrification* is that it is not even a word that translates easily—literally or metaphorically. More importantly, trying to see every displacement everywhere, especially in poorer cities, as just mimicking urban transformation in rich Global North countries replicates colonial analyses yet again:

> What gentrification researchers need to do now is to critically debate the international usefulness of the term "gentrification" and to consider how comparison might take place with respect to historic gentrifications (there are plenty of new histories to be written) and contemporary processes of gentrification in the Global North *and* the Global South. We should not read gentrification in the Global South as simply the recreation of the periphery (the urban South) in the image of the supposed centre (London or New York) . . .
>
> I would like to see "a more inclusive perspective on the geography and history of gentrification," but one informed by the new debates on comparative urbanism . . . I find the social construction of gentrification as "an object of study" increasingly problematic in the face of the mutation of gentrification (e.g. from an urban to a suburban mindset) and its rapid spread in the Global South. I am concerned that traditional conceptualizations of gentrification from the Global North will dominate and thus distort accounts of gentrification in/from the Global South . . .
>
> Of course, extending the term "gentrification" yet again risks it collapsing under the weight of this burden, but as I have argued before this is a risk worth taking.[16]

This is really nicely phrased. Rather than apply a term, or analytical lens, or theoretical perspective blindly or orthodoxically (or doxically for that matter), it befits us to look closely at what's underfoot: what forces are in play, how they operate, and who is being compelled to act. It is certainly true that power imitates power, and global-city enthusiasts and aspirants everywhere look to London and try to replicate or imitate it. The city remains the touchstone whose sun never sets for colonial urban imaginations.

But London is just in a *sui generis* category of one by most significant measures. If it made sense to describe displacements as "gentrification" in London in the mid-1960s, it may well still, but better is to see a fractured and jumbled set of formations. Loretta applied a taxonomy to some of the processes: in "inner London" areas, there are definitely new-build gentrifications underway, but they tend not to be the residential condo-izations so familiar in other cities, mostly the standard glassy towers and starchitectural forays, that are institutional in nature, especially the university, office, and corporate headquarter–type projects.

In other neighborhoods, such as Brixton and Croydon, there are new renditions of "loft living" proliferating—primarily the repurposing of old manufacturing and industrial facilities into swanky apartments. Almost every borough in London outside the core that can assemble enough capital is trying to build high-density nodes, especially around transit centers, as is ubiquitous in Vancouver. London has historically trailblazed with this strategy, and transit-oriented strategies present easy rationales for urban renewal displacements. It is becoming increasingly common for these renewals to require the demolition of council estates. Every neighborhood of London is home to various combinations of these developments, and all are targets of the destruction historically wreaked by the "rent gap," thanks to voracious property investors and homeowners upgrading their properties.

There is no one type of gentrification anywhere, and in such an intensively habited city as London, with fortunes to be made on every block, the competition comes from every direction. Loretta has accurately identified the centrifugally expulsive forces of capital that create banishments from certain centers within London, but these forces also expel people out of the city entirely. Gentrification comes in wildly variegated, blended and layered forms within London, but on top of that, because it is such a dominant city in England, peripheralization often also means lower-incomed residents and jobs are spun out not just to peripheral neighborhoods, but to other, smaller cities. It wouldn't be wrong to view much of the country in toto as sub-urban London, with peripheralized production and resources feeding the central city—a nationally scaled empire.

If this book is trying to make sense of new urban reorderings and sub-urbanizations, what can thinking about London add? My instinct is that even though London is so fundamentally distinct in so many ways, some of the same processes of displacement are in play there, just piled up on another, hybridized and acceler-ated. Understanding what is happening in the cities around us, including cities that are a lot smaller and a lot less complex than London, can't fixate on any single cause or element. Thinking about other cities can offer flashes of insight, but there is some-thing about comparative urbanism that often sniffs of ranking, of a competitive pitting of cities against one another. Analysis across and between cities cannot be a search for universalizing themes or transformations, but to see the multi-directionality of how places echo, appropriate, reconstituted, borrow and reflect each other.

12

In one of my favorite of Loretta's essays, written in 2011 and called "The Geography of Gentrification: Thinking through Comparative Urbanism," she notes:

> In Shanghai nearly a million people have been "relocated" from the central city to the outskirts of the city over the past 12 years and 51.02 million square metres of housing has been demolished . . . The Asian Coalition for Housing Rights has monitored evictions in seven Asian countries (Bangladesh, China, India, Indonesia, Japan, Malaysia and the Philippines) and shown that evictions increased dramatically: between January to June 2004, 334,593 people were evicted in the urban areas of these countries; in January to June 2005, 2,084,388 people were evicted. The major reason for these evictions was/is "the beautification of the city" (read gentrification). In the majority of cases, people did not receive any compensation for the losses they incurred and where resettlement did take place it was 25–60 kilometres from the city centre.

Evictions always come with some putative rationale draped in rhetorical contortions—the city needs beautification, or it will be happier, more livable, more walkable, cleaner, revived, revitalized, renewed, creative or whatever—but at heart those are always arguments about land and power. They are claims for one class of resident or way of being in the world as superior, and thus justified in displacing another. But how that lands, the rationales offered, the stories that get repeated—those all have their own distinctive smells and sounds.

And of course, Surrey is hardly immune to these exact same depredations; it just operates in a slightly more humble fashion than London tends to. It has dawned with some force on local power players just how much money is lying around unsupervised in this unassuming sub-urban soil. As Vancouver spirals into new, baffling levels of housing unaffordability and precarity (the city is going on three decades now firmly ranked in the upper echelons of least affordable places in the world), more and more people are willing to hold their nose, settle their stomachs, and consider investing in this so-called periphery.

The City of Surrey is on a breakneck pace in its development, approving residential towers, especially around SkyTrain stations, about as quickly as planners can give the green light. What was once a dispiritingly tattered quilt of low-end, low-density businesses and institutions is now alive with capital and construction. The sea of vast surface-grade parking lots is being chewed up with development billboards announcing the imminent arrival of yet another many-story, multi-use tower. What was once the haggard neighborhood of Whalley has been energetically rebranded as City Centre. A city core is being built essentially from scratch. A new city hall, central library, university buildings, an art gallery and much else have leapt up, surrounding the extant mall, and bingo! A downtown!

But it's not just the parking lots that are getting consumed, it's acres of low-income housing. Whalley has long been marked by huge expanses of affordable housing stock: mostly developments ranging from three to six stories and twenty to eighty units, all of them full of two- and three-bedroom apartments amenable to families. These were largely built in the 1970s and '80s but have remained a regional escape valve of affordable housing stock that the new City Centre is replacing with fifteen-to-forty-story towers, some of them rentals but mostly condos.

As that cheap housing and cheap commercial spaces get steadily replaced—and new-SkyTrain-proximate rents shoot up —there is a palpable unease throughout Whalley. There are still concentrations of social services, still a lot of street drug activity and homelessness, still a lot of generalized scrappiness, but the smell of the "new Surrey" is in the air. You cannot miss the skyscrapers and the cranes, the haphazard shiny new developments, the constant roadwork—but it's more than that. It's the dispiritingly long lines for buses heading out to Cloverdale and Langley and even further east where new cheap housing clusters beckon. It's the hustle of hustlers sniffing around for development opportunities, the real estate fliers pushed through the mail slot, the dismayed "wait, is Surrey getting gentrified?" jokes.

Everything about Surrey is defined by movement. The decades-long and still explosive population growth here is almost entirely due to in-migration from other parts of the world, and migrants are everything about why Surrey is so alive. That energy is also what is attracting all the new waves of investment and pushing those same lower-income arrivals further afield. Suburbs, and especially new sub-urbs, have always been constrained by highly limited transportation options and huge separating distances—the paucities of public transit, the miles-long blocks, the traffic jams, the low densities. Now, as major public transit infrastructure pushes and probes into Surrey, those new mobility options further peripheralize, displacing poorer people yet another bus ride away.

Surrey boosters energetically celebrate the massive population growth, deploying every possible grim branding cliché about progress ("A City on the Move!"). At the same time the city is seized by narratives of gangs, youth violence, community safety and securitization. Within and without Surrey, it is the first and last thing people inevitably want to talk about, concerns that barely obscure the underlying xenophobia and racialization. The population growth is celebrated and decried in the same breath: some kinds of movement and mobility are reified, others reviled. Change and influx are desperately courted, but not too much change, and with the right kinds of people, lest stability be threatened and the correct order of things slips away.

As Hagar Kotef writes, subject positions are always related to mobility: movement is itself subject forming. Some kinds of movement are understood as freedom, others as a threat:

> Movement has been conceptualized and has materialized within sets of material, racial, geographic, and gendered conditions in a way that allowed only some subjects to appear as free when moving (and as oppressed when hindered). The movement (or

hindrance) of other subjects has been configured differently. Colonized subjects who were declared to be nomads, poor who were seen as vagabond or thrown into vagrancy as they lost access to lands, women whose presumed hysterical nature was attached to their inability to control bodily fluids, all were constituted (or rather deconstituted) as unruly subjects whose movement is a problem to be managed.[17]

The liberal subject and liberal society are formed by commitments to freedom of movement but co-produce certain limited kinds of mobilities alongside enclosures, evictions, constraints and imprisonments. Movement is the justification for non-liberal moments and spaces within liberal regimes, and sub-urbs are created, constituted and re-constituted by constant movement and the regulation of mobilities.

This is precisely what John Washington was telling me in Portland, where Black populations have been constantly shuffled and moved along, constrained in one neighborhood, then displaced to another, then dispersed. "You need to be asking, what is driving this conduct? Black people have always moved and migrated . . . Sure, people are moving, but what's the underlying force?" I think back to my time in Ferguson and Kinloch and about movement and hindrances on subjects, and what Ferguson organizer Inez Bordeaux said after that ArchCity Defenders training session: "Who keeps us safe? *We* keep us safe!"

13

There's another version of this book in some alternate universe where I visit other cities, in China and the Global South, and meet with scholars and activists there to extend my comparative analysis, to ask after generalizable patterns and divergences. I had plans in 2020 to visit Shanghai and Chennai, India, and had written a partial chapter about Toronto, but that year had other plans for all of us.

Instead, post-pandemic, I called up Fulong Wu, who is the Bartlett Professor of Planning at University College London and has produced prolific research about peri-urban development throughout the world, very often writing and editing with Roger Keil. A significant amount of his work explores urban and suburban China, and more specifically, Shanghai, and I was curious about whether anything about what sees in China travels theoretically.

Fulong focuses a lot of his work on governance, and one of the first things he told me was that in China, the city historically has been inside the state and thus integral to its planning structure, while the countryside, substantively outside the state, has not been part of that structure and thus been largely self-contained and left to self-organize. That traditional dualism has been a challenge for the development of a land market and the rapid conversion of agricultural areas to urban and peri-urban uses, with a mélange of actors jostling and elbowing one another across suburban interface zones.

The historic urban–rural divide is being breached from all directions in these newly constituted intertidal, peri-urban landscapes. From wealthier urban residents buying land for second homes, to poorer urbanites being relocated to huge affordable housing projects, to farmers building informal housing for migrant workers, to huge conglomerates constructing new industrial parks, Chinese peri-urbanism has acquired much of the same messy, jumbled and uncertain character of so many North American sub-urbs.

Unlike most places, though, the Chinese government is flexing its considerable muscle with a variety of multi-modal approaches, developing planned "new towns," allowing a certain degree of messy improvisation, and strategically deploying a bouquet of market mechanisms across new suburban frontiers, confluent with new regimes of state-entrepreneurialism. The mélange of settlement and development morphologies across Chinese suburbs reflects the maw of competing interests and administrative zones, and Fulong's descriptions definitely remind me of Surrey, which shows some evidence of coherent planning, though only every once in a while.

Fulong also noted that these patterns of highly fragmented peri-urban landscapes marked by zones of integration into urban systems are the expression of distinct fragmented systems of land governance that often bypass local municipalities. Huge new accumulation nodes of global connectivity are being built across Chinese peri-urban landscapes, but these tend to skip past communities and operate outside their control. Fulong, who has also done considerable comparative analysis, observes echoes of these variegated, splintered and brawling suburban characteristics in China across African and Asian sub-urbs of all kinds, with few obviously stable forms evident.[18]

This seems to support my proposition that the defining character of peripheral, or peri-urban, areas is movement. The sub-urbs that I know feel markedly different from their more stable, settled core cities—there is still so much up for grabs, with people and capital sloshing in and out, various actors grasping whatever they can, trying to drive a stake in the ground, so little easily legible.

The historically informed ideal of the city has always revolved around difference, the aspirational liberal notion that cities are magnets for everyone who has escaped stultifying small towns or families to find sweet relief in the fluid social and cultural mobilities of the city.

That still feels true in lots of ways, in lots of places. Everyone knows the thrill, the spark of being on a crowded street, the cacophony, the flows that keep bringing something new. But in place after beloved place, that ideal seems less real and more imaginary: the urban imagination has calcified and been captured by banality.

Someone might call the movement of working-class and racialized people to sub-urbs 'retreat', but mostly it feels like *refusal*. I want to think and theorize about that movement, as flows and tides, of illegibilities and revolt. I want to know how new forms of social organizing are possible in sub-urbs and what we can learn from thinking through movements and circulations, because to my eyes that refusal seems full of hopefulness.

Part 3

SEEING LIKE A SUB-URB

We experience life as a continuity, and only after it falls away, after it becomes the past, do we see its discontinuities. The past, if there is such a thing, is mostly empty space, great expanses of nothing, in which significant persons and events float.

—Teju Cole, *Open City*

1

My grandmother, Joan Trottier—"Gan," to us—was born in 1919 and died in 2021: she lived from pandemic to pandemic. For almost all of her 102 years, and right up until her final year of decline, she was amazingly sturdy: going for long walks every day, swimming, gardening, slurping G&Ts, playing bridge and crib, beefing constantly. Her long-lasting, robust health was largely due to the devoted care of her children, especially my mother, but her constitutional hardiness was a product of general pugnacity, stubbornness and a deep will to dominate.

I spent most of my childhood living in her house, one that she ruled with a firm fist. I have internalized so many of her life lessons so deeply, I would have no idea how to dislodge them, particularly the ones about how to be healthy. Her prescriptions for haleness form a kind of hyper-Waspy attitude toward physical and mental well-being: keep the windows open during the day to encourage the circulation of air, clean relentlessly, take brisk walks outside frequently, work every day so you sleep well at night, keep a stiff upper lip, take no medicines unless absolutely necessary, and fresh seawater will cure most anything.

Central to her teachings was a strong aversion to complaints. Griping, grievance, or whining was evidence of a soft mind, and a weak mentality bred a weak body. One of her most frequent reproaches was, "Don't be soft in the head, boy!" Once, as a child, I ran to her crying after a neighborhood scrap. Her response: "Matthew, nobody likes a tattletale."

When Gan was a child growing up in North Vancouver, she was diagnosed with a rare hip condition called Perthes disease and, in the late 1920s, the prescription for it was immediate hospitalization with her leg in traction. She spent more than eighteen months—from ages eleven to thirteen—with her lower half immobilized. For most of that time she was forced to do everything—from eating to homework to bathing—while lying flat on her back, as weighted pullies, hanging from her knees and pulling her feet downward, released tension on her hip to allow it to recover correctly.

She spent that year and a half far from home, in the Queen Alexandra Solarium for Crippled Children, on Vancouver Island.[1] The solarium was the first children's health facility in British Columbia, built for kids battling chronic and long-term illnesses, part of the historical wave of health establishments that birthed the sanatorium movement. The Queen Alexandra was a vast, lodge-like medical/convalescent structure with a huge covered porch overlooking the ocean. Every day, the children—Gan included—were wheeled outside in their beds so that they could get fresh sea air and enjoy the view, based on the prescription that resting in circulating air was the cure for a whole swath of diseases and debilitations.

Starting at the end of the nineteenth century and through to the middle of the twentieth century, sanatoria were common across North America and Europe, and eventually globally. The movement was prompted by the widespread prevalence and lethality of tuberculosis, but sanatoria were prescribed to treat everything from asthma, rheumatism and emotional exhaustion to alcoholism, hysteria and masturbation. The core tenets of sanatoria practice revolved around a precisely calibrated mix of movement and immobilization. Sanatoria were located in what were understood as healthy climates, almost always in the countryside, often at high altitude, or in the desert.

The first arguments for sanatoria were made in the 1840s by British physician George Bodington, who claimed that the orthodox treatment of consumption with hospitalizations and rounds of drugs was useless and that only rest and a healthy climate were effective. His analysis and proposed treatment were widely adopted by the end of the century, with patients undergoing long periods of extremely sedentary rest, often up to a year or more, supplemented with as much exposure to healthy air as possible.

Patients were expected to spend many hours every day out on porches—or solariums—that ran the full length of buildings and were entirely open to the elements. The more time they spent outside the better, sometimes 24–7 regardless of weather, resting in warm beds doing and moving as little as possible, letting the air expand and strengthen the lungs. As patients got healthier, they were proscribed increasingly vigorous doses of outdoor exercise.

The sanatorium movement dissolved in the mid-1950s, after the discovery of antibiotics that dealt with tuberculosis extremely effectively, but the basic pillars of that philosophy have remained, reconstituted and rearranged in various forms and places, and certainly in my own body. My grandmother was cured in the solarium —a kind of miracle, given that she spent ninety more years moving constantly and I never heard word of any real hip problems. The lessons of the solarium have been corporally learned through generations of my family—including my own children—passing, telephone-game style, in constantly shifting forms.

All her life, Gan told us to turn the heat way down at night and tuck ourselves under extra blankets if we are cold. We should get out for a brisk walk early in the morning and move around whenever possible through the day. Children should go outside to play and run around but, when in the house, should be quiet and sedentary. Sitting and reading is good; watching TV is bad, shameful even. Manual labor is encouraged, especially gardening or farming, but only as a hobby; white-collar jobs are always the aspiration. Exercise is strongly promoted, and being overweight is the worst. But being too thin is a sign of anxiety and weakness. Cleanliness and sanitation should be attended to constantly and with vigor.

All of this, of course, is a recipe for ordering certain kinds of bodies, and in my family's case, is aggressively inflected at every step by whiteness. We are settlers: my grandma was born here in Metro Vancouver, not long after her parents arrived. Gan's father, my great-grandfather, was a British sea captain who worked out of the North Vancouver port, and her entire childhood was spent carving out a new life on the colonial frontier. Her ethics and philosophy of movement were striated by tensions between mobility and constraint, constriction and circulation, with some kinds of movement venerated, others reviled.

As an enthusiastic colonial subject, Gan was commanded to set an example: the taming of the wilderness and the natives mimicked the taming and disciplining of one's own life. Bodies and societies alike should be orderly, scrubbed clean, vigorous, disciplined and primed for progress. If, as per Hannah Arendt, movement is "the substance and meaning of all things political," then I can easily trace the ideas I associate closely with freedom to my understanding of movement.

2

It's no surprise that Gan was so interested in the circulation of air, water and flesh.

Her mother, Gertrude—a.k.a. Gee—was born in 1882 in England, at the height of the Victorian era when the country was grappling with the urban repercussions of the Industrial Revolution.

The rapid Eurospheric industrialization and mechanization of the nineteenth century triggered such explosive population growth and urbanization that England grew from eight to thirty million people in just that century. Many of those people abandoned small towns and rural lifestyles for urban factory jobs—so many, in fact, that London had leapt from one to six million people by 1900. This unprecedented and unimagined flood of urban migrants created catastrophic overcrowding: slums and brutal housing and working conditions that overwhelmed municipal service capacities.

The density of urban Victorian poverty birthed floods of disease, primarily waterborne due to the marked absence of sewage treatment options. Cholera, smallpox, typhus, tuberculosis and a host of other diseases found welcome conditions in a city where vast numbers of horses were used for all means of transportation, each day producing mountains of manure with few means of disposal. On top of the animal wastes, raw human sewage flowed—directly or through leaky or patchwork piping—into ditches, creeks and streets, with vast amounts ending up in the Thames, either by accident or through deliberate dumping, where the tide sloshed it upriver and onto banks.

These grimly unsanitary conditions were exacerbated by the proliferation of new factories and the widespread use of coal-burning stoves in homes, producing thick and heavy air throughout the city, adding to the everyday sewage gases that seeped back into homes via sinks, toilets and baths. With working residents crammed together in increasingly crowded conditions, very often with no windows or ventilation, it is no surprise that elites throughout England panicked.

In the fevered imagination of city fathers, the deprivation and poverty of Victorian slums corresponded with a general collapse of morality that threatened the whole country. Nightmarish visions of crime, sexual depravity, family collapse and violence were breathlessly debated in the press, Parliament and parlor rooms. More ominous was the looming social discord, revolt and revolution that would surely follow if conditions were not ameliorated, and, in a time of energetic socialist and anarchist organizing, this threat was not just performative pearl-clutching.

It was clear that Victorian sanitation was at the heart of the problem and the free movement of liquids and air had to be regulated. A newly constrained population—working and living in dense confinement in flats and factories—desperately needed new forms of circulation. Out of this cauldron emerged the practice of modern urban planning, and with it a raft of new schemes to disperse and declutter the city: the Garden City and City Beautiful movements, Le Corbusier's Contemporary City, Haussmann's cleansing of Paris, and many other models, all driven by the imperative to humanize urban conditions, to spread out urban settlements, to extend the city further out into the country and to bring more of the countryside into cities via parks and landscaping.

These precursors laid the intellectual and planning groundwork for modern suburbanizations. The connective tissue holding it together is mobility: dispersing urban residential populations outward only works if there are vehicles for moving people. The desire to plan and organize mobilities—the ability for some to freely move between city and country via transit and cars—opened up new possibilities for surplus labor extraction. Wealthy classes could move out of the city to breathe freely while profiting from the dense productivity of industrial labor. At the same time, working classes could be relocated to peripheries to ameliorate dire living conditions and ensure a functionally healthy workforce.

My ancestors carried with them this visceral history of Victorian Europe, trying to shed the stench of industrialization in Ireland, England, France and Scotland. As they worked their way across the New World, with my great-grandparents settling on Canada's far west coast, the frontier beckoned with a blank canvas to work with and new possibilities for ordering movement.

The first order of business here in North America was expelling and confining Indigenous people: first removing them from their territories, organizing them within a reservation system and capturing their children in residential schools. Settlers disrupted and foreclosed traditional hunting, fishing and trapping patterns, while interrupting seasonal patterns of migrations to fish camps and hunting grounds, all within a Lockean legal framework of property ownership and stable settlement.

The next step was to build out an immigration system that could bolster and expand the settler population, thereby occupying Indigenous territory with a productive populace. Some kinds of immigrants—Chinese and Japanese especially, here on the West Coast—were provisionally welcomed as labor for railway construction and resource extraction, but that welcome was rescinded whenever necessary, with people expelled or confined in internment camps. Others were welcomed with far more open arms and offered free land to work and sprawling new sceneries to defile.

The liberal subject of North American democracy was constituted by a freedom to move and the cleansing of others from those landscapes. The open frontiers allowed for a restless mobility in search of land, resources and economic opportunities: a cowboy horizon to shake off the Old World cobwebs. North American cities were informed by the same logics—older cities along the Eastern Seaboard in the maw of industrialization were enacting intense concentration for some people, and rapid dispersion of others.

North American settler colonialism is a wide-ranging exercise in ordering via circulation and the lack thereof. My ancestors' movements, as much as mine, are predicted on the confinement of others'.

Among the key justifications for colonization is the imperative of progress. Primitive, backwater and uncivilized areas are beset with a double affliction in the eyes of colonists: simultaneous economic and cultural stagnation exacerbated by an excess of bodily movement and failure to settle. Progress requires spurring societies along for their own good, while restraining and limiting surplus mobility. Development has to proceed at the correct pace, with a normal amount of movement balanced with stability and security. This is settlement.

3

I grew up in the countryside, with few real neighbors. Gan and her husband purchased land on Patricia Bay in 1958 for $8,000. After my grandfather died in 1963, she used the insurance money to build a house, moving out permanently in 1970. The house was a modest rancher-cottage, perched right on the edge of the ocean, the property spilling down onto a spectacular beach, surrounded by forest and blackberries. The neighborhood was a little white enclave, with all three of its roads out passing through Indigenous reservations.

My parents, brother and I first lived on the other side of the bay, moving in with Gan in 1980 after our rent became unaffordable. I had spent much of my childhood in her house already; she was our primary caregiver when our parents were at work or school, so it was an obvious move. The idea that we were a rural family was baked into our collective self-mythologizing. My parents were post-Beat, pre-hippie adherents to Gary Snyder, with a back-to-the-land, healthy-living dogma that neatly dovetailed with Gan's pretensions to owning a country estate. Both parties were opposed to clogged, dirty city life and wanted to get far from the madding crowd's ignoble strife.

Over the next few decades, our neighborhood smoothly charted its teleological arc from rural enclave to upscale suburb as the city of Victoria stretched north, and the old house is now surrounded by limp, mostly empty semi-modern semi-mansions, moldering quietly. All of these versions of the neighborhood aggressively embittered me, and so I left as soon as possible: a young man straight off the turnip truck, drawn wide-eyed to every city I could get to.

Cities were everything my desiccated little corner of the world was so lacking. They were fast, chippy, and full of all kinds of people and buildings and ideas I had never imagined. I also quickly adhered to the idea that cities were ecologically sustainable in their very density: more people living on a smaller footprint and sharing resources. That rendition of urban ecology has become functional planning orthodoxy: sprawl is the devil, eating up agricultural land with porcine gluttony, requiring highways, cars and giant housing tracts. Density is the salve to suburban sprawl: enough people living in close proximity makes walking, biking and transiting possible.

In this respect, contemporary urban planning has taken a sharp U-turn over the past several decades, running in precisely the opposite direction from the first century of planning history. Old ideas of dispersing and decluttering the city have been overtaken by "smart" planning, complete communities, and the increasingly alarming velocity of global warming. With this about-face, the idea of the hinterland has been revived in new guises—a German word meaning "the land behind," or all that area outside the urban—which is designated as un-urban but still tasked with feeding the city with raw materials and people, and receiving in return the detritus, the garbage, and the waste.

These two renditions of urban concentration and dispersal are closely wedded to ideas of circulation, both of goods and people, and simultaneously of emplacement. Both have long colonial histories of settlement and fixity, and the proper ordering of human bodies. In each case, human togetherness is driven by the liberal desire for both mobility and settlement, and notions about who deserves to be where.

Growing up on Vancouver Island, it never crossed my mind that our moving there was a problem. It never occurred to me that we were settlers. It was impossible to miss the intense Indigenous poverty all around us, but that was just the way things were. I took a bus to and from high school, and at the end of every school day there were two buses parked out front—one for Indigenous kids and one for settlers. We lined up in long queues beside each other, each line never paying the other much attention, and we boarded the buses at the same time. There was only one road, and the two buses traveled it one behind the other, each stopping and waiting as passengers disembarked at their stops, the Indigenous kids getting off on reserve land, everyone else everywhere else. Even though I was a political kid, I never noticed we were living in an apartheid state.

Gan complained often and bitterly about the reservations. At heart she was mostly a kind and generous person, and over time, many of her most abject prejudices calmed, but never those against Indigenous people. Even though she knew that the frankly racist views she used to recite to us were no longer acceptable in public, she could not let go of her loathing of Indigenous communities. Primary among her grievances was the condition of homes on the reservation, the garbage on the lawns, the old cars and appliances out front, the supposedly dirty clothes and hair of the children. She could not understand why they would not clean their properties up, and that lack of tidiness was as damning a trait as she could imagine.

She made it clear to us that Indigenous reservations were specific kinds of contamination and pollution. Our family had moved to the country onto clean land to find healthy lifestyles and escape the filth of the modern city. While Indigenous people had to be restrained to make way for settlers, they also needed to adapt to the correct speed of progress and movement. It is this commitment to proper forms of circulation that I was raised to understand as home.

I miss my grandma every day. I miss her fierce will, I miss playing endless crib games with her, I miss her cackle, I miss the profound heliocentric force she exerted on all our family. I still sneeze just like her, am overbearing just like her, know a little about gardening, believe that saltwater cures everything, always try to stiff-upper-lip it, enthusiastically enjoy tea time. I am her grandson. I am not shy to celebrate everything I owe her and my love for her, but I'd better not be shy to acknowledge the stains on my history and character that she is part of.

4

It is in this context that am I thinking about the settler city and the settler sub-urb. I am curious about how my own colonial heritage and presence infects how I see fixities and movements. I am curious about how ideologies of circulation have built urbanist orthodoxies. Is the idea of settlement—of staying in one physical place over an extended time—necessarily a colonial construction? Is that the core rationale for occupation, for possession, for converting land into property?

I want to return to that pervasive sensibility threading through ecological thinking (and so often in so many other strains of thinking) that lionizes rootedness. The argument is that staying in a physical location over duration is the key to caring for a place, and for a long time I generally and mostly unthinkingly accepted that claim. I now think that stance is incorrect but also dangerous. The argument easily falls apart upon even the most cursory prodding, but it is both pervasive and powerful, and easily bleeds into racist environmental arguments that migrants can never care for a place properly and never experience the same deep love and attachment that people who have been there longer embody. It is also a political position that undergirds so much so-called progressive urbanist thinking and planning.

The fetishizations of local community show up in many different forms. Cities in the Global North are habitually ensnared by bourgeois attempts at "placemaking," "urban villages," and similar tropes. The general idea is that while cities may be huge, roiling masses of people generating anomie, isolation and loneliness, that lack of community can be mitigated by building mini-villages within cities via urban design features like cob-house bus shelters, murals, parklets and free libraries housed in sweet, little faux-cottages on street corners.

There's always something appealing about these placemaking initiatives. They speak to a sweet, nostalgic, hearth-and-home version of community that feels like a warm cup of tea. But in practice they tend to be cloyingly twee, predominantly white NIMBY exercises that inscribe a very particular middle-class rendition of community. They often have something of a *terra nullis* vibe: Was there no place there before you all started "making" it? In practice, "placemaking" happens after the working-class people who actually make the place function have been moved along, and long after any Indigenous presence has been erased.

I do believe that dense, walkable communities are a worthy ideal, at whatever scale. I think settlements of all sizes have to confront climate change in all their constructions. But my encounters with sub-urbs have thrown all my ideas about what that might look like into disarray. How can we see sub-urban residents not as outcasts or helpless victims of capital, and cities not as places beset by constant loss and escape and displacement and expulsion? How can we see other forces shaping the city and sub-urb? Can we construct an alternative urban cartography, to see and map the city differently—literally, socially and metaphorically?

I think this requires that we celebrate both rootedness and mobilities at the same time. Most white people can always pick up and move. White people like me think we come from nowhere and belong everywhere and thus deserve to be able to go anywhere we feel like, even if someone is already there. Colonial regulation of movement sees Indigenous, migrant and poor people as embodying a surplus of movement, of moving too much, and in the wrong ways, requiring specific ordering to achieve the right balance. Certain migrants are welcome to travel when their labor is needed, but not when they compete for jobs with settlers. People are forced to move in the name of development when they are in the way of progress but constrained when they move too much and into the wrong neighborhoods.

Colonial occupation is simultaneously the calcification of mobility and settlement: an expansionist desire for constant movement to new land, and a refusal to leave territory that has been captured. Indigenous and racialized inhabitants are burdened by a similar double bind: simultaneously moving too much, in all the wrong ways; and not moving enough, in all the wrong ways.

Colonizers can see the surplus value in land, how it can be profited from, what can be extracted. The colonized do not deserve to stay on the land because they are wasting it, not deploying it sufficiently. This is a key Lockean rationale for New World occupation: Indigenous inhabitants are not only being wasteful by not settling down and working the land correctly, but they are also actually being greedy by wandering across it so promiscuously. By not enclosing land, resuscitating it as property and subjecting it to industry, Indigenous hunter-gatherer-trappers are selfishly denying the most productive use of all the land to the rest of humanity.

The property-accumulation axis is central to understanding the so-called correct balance of movement and settlement. By their very nature, colonial states efface pluralities of relations and identities—they demand adherence to a single transcendent identity: the propertied citizen. Indigenous inhabitants and migrants alike refuse that stable designation by both moving too much and too little, either actually or metaphorically. The regulation of movement is both preceded by and (re)forms identities. As Kotef writes:

> The movement of subjects—which is always given in this dialectic of myth and reality, of possibilities and actualizations—partakes in the formation of bodies. Put differently, schemas of identity are formed in tandem with schemas of mobility . . .
>
> Assumptions of difference—economic, gendered, racial—have long provided such a justification for exclusionary practice and violence. Yet the more a regime perceives itself to be egalitarian, the more reluctant it is to draw on identity categories in order to justify different principles of governance. One cannot be arrested simply because he is black; one cannot be denied suffrage simply because she is a woman; one's village cannot be demolished simply because

she does not belong to the Jewish majority in Israel. Patterns of mobility have functioned, and still do, to convert these identities into punishable (criminal, as well as pathological) practices.[2]

I am wondering how we can think of cities as constantly shifting, reordering and unfixed—and celebrate movements and mobilities, rather than decrying them? How can we build new ways of seeing the city and urban organizing with a more nuanced view of the relationships between emplacement and mobility? I ask because if can we dispense of any easy definitions about where cities start and stop, what their proper form is, and the concept of the city as a unified settled whole unit, then I think we have a better base for fighting back against racial capitalism. Movement and fixity are never independent, they are relational: one person's ease of movement always constrains someone else's. Someone's claim to place denies another's claim. Someone's desire for rootedness forces someone else to keep moving.

We can celebrate movements and refusals in the same breath. Anti-colonial resistances take many forms and are always expressed in nuance, plurality and relationality. Consider how Indigenous resistance and migrant justice movements alike both act as antidotes to settler insistences on fixed sovereignties, coming from very different directions, but each defying racial capital's insistence on disciplining movement.

One of Yellowknives Dene scholar Glen Coulthard's most powerful contributions to anti-colonial theory is the idea of *grounded normativity*, which he deploys to explain what fundamentally distinguishes Indigenous relations with land from colonial insistence on property—a relationship to the land and others expressed in flexible territoriality and porous sovereignties:

> One of the negative effects of this power-laden process of discursive translation has been a reorientation of the meaning of self-determination for many (but not all) Indigenous people in the North; a reorientation of Indigenous struggle from one that was once deeply *informed* by the land as a system of reciprocal relations and obligations (grounded normativity), which in turn informed our critique of capitalism in the period examined above,

to a struggle that is now increasingly *for* land, understood now as material resource to be exploited in the capital accumulation process.[3]

This is a critical differentiation that can speak specifically to urban struggles. It is a call to think relationally about movement, land and place, and at the same time to refuse to see land as a resource, as raw material. This is not, though, a set of ideas that comes easy to settlers like me.

One of my very favorite books growing up was Defoe's *Robinson Crusoe*. There were very few kids, or people in general, living nearby, so I spent a lot of time on my own, and self-contained, autonomous settlerdom was an easy fantasy to slide into. It was an obvious extension of the family mythology of us living in the country. I used to pack a bunch of blankets, Asterix comic books and snacks and wander down the beach, build a fort out of driftwood and then hole up in there for hours. I'd occasionally get ambitious and build a stockade for my imaginary goats, stash a pile of rocks to defend against attack, and heroically find ways to survive.

It's a blunt metaphor, but it is easy to notice how frontierism seeps into my everyday thinking about property and place and home. I am of Waspy stock, and the idea that a man's home is his castle, the place to pull up the drawbridge and defend at all costs, is entangled with my beliefs about who I am and should be; it's a common trope writ social, writ national. I can see how attractively pervasive mythologies of self-reliance are to me, and how eager I am to describe myself as an independent, self-made man in control of myself and my destiny, despite all evidence to the contrary.

5

What if most urban theory has been seeing the city entirely from the wrong angle—fetishizing some kinds of centers and pitying those that are outside that? What if that is just one more neo-colonial ordering? What if new sub-urbs celebrated movement, adjustment, non-fixities and mobilities in the same ways that migrant justice movements celebrate new arrivals? What if sub-urbs are not bereft, sad places of refuge that people have fled to, but vibrant places of refusal and regeneration?

The fetishization of a romanticized urban form is not a particularly new phenomenon, but it sure has accelerated over the past few decades. The pacification and cleansing of inner cities have opened up new possibilities for capital, and I am not sure anyone anticipated just how profitable condoization would become, although it is bound up with urbanists' myopia.

If we get stuck in a predictably twee vision of what a city could and should be for, and what a "proper" city looks like, we lose sight of what is actually happening. Contemporary bourgeois urbanism is enthralled by a specific, nostalgic city form, maybe something like a little village in Italy with swanky technology: charming brick buildings, town squares surrounded with cafés, walkable shopping, bike lanes, lovely backyard gardens, well-dressed people with graduate degrees and liberal politics casually "working" over mid-day bottles of wine.

I am episodically highly attracted to this vision of a city. It's enthralling in an embarrassingly snooty, Eurospheric way. But it's all Disney. Look again, and everything that makes these urban pockets of so-called "real" city life actually work is happening well outside the city walls. Take Vancouver, which is widely celebrated (especially by its own designers) for its startling inner-city regeneration. The Vancouver experiment is supposedly a dramatic success in drawing residents downtown, densifying with podium towers and building compact neighborhoods.

At first glance, that is totally true: there is a dense, walkable character to the urban core. But look again, and really, the vast bulk of the city is just a huge, sprawling single-family-home mess. And look a little further out, to, say, Surrey, and you will find that all the people who do the actual work of making the city run are relegated far, far from those attractive city accoutrements. It's a Vegas trick of facades, distraction and sleight of hand.

It is impossible to separate Manhattan from Trenton or Jersey City or Paterson or Canarsie. Or to separate Paris or Quito or Cape Town or wherever from the seas of working-class and migrant workers who are assiduously ordered outside the gates. It's easy to deride the callousness of Qatar or Dubai, which shamelessly imports laborers from Bangladesh and Pakistan and warehouses them in tent camps while they build gleaming cities for penny wages. At least Qatar and Dubai aren't trying to hide the real cost of their cities.

One of the great victories of *The Dawn of Everything*, the lauded 2021 book by David Wengrow and David Graeber, is that it takes an axe to the closed hermeneutical arguments about what cities are. The authors assemble a huge volume of multi-continental archaeological evidence to suggest that there is an incredible range of human settlements that do not adhere to easy extant urban/non-urban categories.

They document some of the earliest versions of cities, including vast regional zones of settlement along the Black Sea, older than the earliest known Mesopotamian cities, that contained many thousands of people. The research was largely obscured from the West during the Cold War, but when these areas were documented, they were never designated as cities—they were called "mega-sites" or "overgrown villages"—because they were huge and sprawling, in one case extending over three hundred hectares. They also had a paucity of centralized facilities and gathering places, and even lacked centralized government or administrative authorities that cities are presumed to need, and thus were relegated to something other, less notable, less historic than so-called "proper" early cities.

Wengrow and Graeber go on to document an incredible amount of variety in the structure, organization, scale and cartography of early settlements, and conclude that there is no one-way street of history, that people have always experimented and lived in all kinds of configurations. There is a long line of contentious debate over whether agriculture begot cities or vice versa, and James Scott has long argued that despots and kings always love settled agriculture, and that the rise of the authoritarian taxing, conscripting state is closely linked to the sedentary form of settlement required by agriculture. But *The Dawn of Everything* shows that early grain states in the Americas had strong egalitarian features that defy the supposed causal link between agriculture and centralized domination.[4]

There is no path-dependent way for cities to grow or contract or shift. There are no thresholds that we cannot retreat from. We are not innately *anything*, and neither are cities. Any teleological stories about cities are all wrong—there is no one developmental path for human settlements. There is always room for playfulness, freedom to escape, freedom to disobey, freedom to imagine a social otherwise.

Urbanist arguments for what a "good" city looks like are not descriptive; they are prescriptive, and mostly designed to lock certain kinds of power in place. There's no requisite arc from hunter-gatherer society to village to town to city to megalopolis to smart city or whatever. History is asymmetrical and messy and unpredictable, with fits and starts and backwaters and eddies and reimagining: we can always think otherwise from what appears inevitable. We are not saddled with a future of constant urban, peripheralized displacements and evictions. There are other cities in our futures.

6

When Selena and I decided to leave the old neighborhood, it was just as much a shock to us as it was to our friends and neighbors. We had lived in one spot essentially all our adult lives. We moved to Commercial Drive in East Vancouver in 1991 and raised a family, living in a series of houses all within a couple of blocks of each other, ending up in one we rented for almost twenty-five years. A bunch of my books were overtly about that neighborhood, and together as a family we wrote a book about the park we lived beside.[5] For almost three decades, all my community organizing was centered in East Van, and I ran schools, youth centers, festivals and events throughout the neighborhood. We were classic Chalfenesque, do-gooder white people fixtures. We knew people and people knew us, we had friends on every block, courted righteous controversies, and knew our place in the world.

But then I started working in Surrey, spending all my waking hours there, stumbling home from the train in the dark every day. And then Selena went back to school, became a prof and started working in Edmonton, traveling back and forth on an academic's schedule. And then the kids all grew up and left home, some far away, and those that stayed in town and moved out struggled to find affordable rent nearby.

As our connections to the neighborhood frayed, the stories we told ourselves about who we were slowly distanced themselves from reality. But it still seemed far-fetched that we might leave the neighborhood, because we barely knew anything else. And leave for the fucking suburbs? Selena and I got a hotel for a weekend in Surrey, a glass box on the eleventh floor, looking down on a sea of immense parking lots, wide-laned roads, and hardly anyone on the streets. We looked at each other blankly, trying to imagine.

We drove around, looking for plausible neighborhoods to live in, and listened to that Courtney Barnett song about her moving out to a suburb called Preston. We got on Craigslist and started scheming. We had no idea what we were looking for, but whatever that was, we didn't see it. Everything was either a one-bedroom in a tower, a four-to-five-bedroom rancher or a basement in one of those ranchers. We talked about how one of those houses would have fit us fifteen years ago, and how, fifteen years from now, maybe we'll fit in one of those little apartments.

When we first moved onto Commercial Drive decades ago now, it was a little barren. There were a ton of houses and apartments available; the streets were pretty quiet—most everything closed down by nine. It was a good, working-class neighborhood, popular with organizers and activists because it was so cheap, had good coffee and was lugging around a highly dubious reputation as being a little dangerous. That reputation served the very-welcome function of keeping rents low.

Over our thirty-year occupancy, the city exploded, fueled by (what else?) a world's fair, the Olympics, and a free-for-all real estate market frenzy. And East Van grew right along with it. Scores of restaurants, clothing stores and bars crab-bucketed each other frantically, creating a constant commercial churn. Festivals and events and artists got the place hopping at night, students started pouring in and it became a hot, edgy real estate landing spot. For a minute it was still cheaper than downtown or the westside, then suddenly got out of control and turned into one of the most expensive and competitive housing markets in the region. You know the drill.

And there is no question that we were part of that. We did so much community work and started so many projects, big and small, some that petered out and many that thrived and lasted. We were significant actors in making the neighborhood more attractive, and thus we are heavily implicated in its demise. It is one of the great ironies of urban activism that any community that organizes and becomes more functional, livelier, sexier makes itself vulnerable to gentrification. Everything that makes a place better puts it at risk.

It is an inevitability that everyone understands in their gut. Sooner or later, you'll have to move. The question is how to time that and when to get out, how to get ahead of the curve. Some people are always able to stay: corral a rent-controlled place, get into a housing co-op, maybe buy something. The danger is that you might be marooned, stuck in a place while everyone and everything that made you want to stay moves on. I've seen this happen to several brilliant community organizations: they develop in a low-income community, do amazing work and are successful enough to buy a building, then look up and realize that the populations they work with have moved far away. I've visited projects in multiple cities that are facing exactly this: they were once community- or neighborhood-based, but most everyone they serve now has to travel an hour or more via transit to reach them.

We didn't want to be those people who got marooned: those tiresome old people telling bitter, old war stories about the way the old neighborhood used to be. We knew we had to move; our landlord just kept raising the rent steadily, and we were living on borrowed time there. But we were exactly those middle-class white people who were the problem in the first place, and now we are exactly those middle-class white people who can so easily pick up and move. Are we just going to fuck up every place we land in?

In 2022 Surrey was named the most dangerous city in Canada.[6] Apparently some organization named Numbeo ranked us No. 53 globally, just "ahead" on the crime index of Almaty, Kazakhstan (54), and Dhaka, Bangladesh (55), but just behind Houston, Texas (52).[7] That kind of project smacks of hysterical bullshit and the same old xenophobia, but whatever. To rank that high is something of a point of badass pride, a macho flex for some. Maybe that inoculates Surrey a little from capital? Could it ever be gentrified? Well sure, and parts already are. And who would lead that charge? People like us.

We ended up buying a float house one suburb over from Surrey, south of Vancouver. It was kind of a weird move, made in the fog of the pandemic, but one we have come to love. Our house bobs ups and down on the Fraser River, our marina looking like a floating trailer park; we are in an overwhelmingly Asian community (there is an "ethnic" aisle in our local grocery with mustard and mayonnaise and stuff in it), and even with our mortgage and moorage costs, we are still paying less than our old rent. We don't own any land, so the house is not technically real estate property. I bragged about this as some kind of settler loophole—that maybe somehow, we were not occupying Indigenous territory because we were on the water, so my smug posturing was ideologically intact. Turns out, though, that the legal description of our house is "chattel," which seems equally ugly, if not worse, and of course we are living on unceded, occupied xʷməθkʷəy̓əm waters. I stopped bragging so much on that point.

Now I am a suburb-to-sub-urb commuter and I barely ever go downtown or to the old neighborhood, maybe once every couple of weeks for drinks or to see a show. The commuting is disorienting and still surprises me every day. There is no functional public transit between Richmond and Surrey, so I am now logging a ton of driving time: a little more than a half hour each way, mostly on a highway. Like everyone else, I listen to sports podcasts, make phone calls and hope that I don't run into too much traffic. I occasionally find that distance sort of awkward, but I like to think of myself as a part of Surrey, as a Surreyite. I'm not "from" there, but I spend pretty much all my waking hours in Surrey, and it feels like that's where all my fidelities are. But I go home to sleep well outside the municipal borders. So then what?

I do not feel particularly bereft at having to leave the neighborhood where we raised our family and put so much heart into. It's not true that we "had" to move. We were not "displaced," even though maybe we might wedge ourselves into that designation if we were being especially righteous. We were not evicted (although a couple times almost were), and we moved mostly of our own volition. We could have stayed and figured it out. We have options and incomes; we are not victims here. Moving has been more than a fine decision: it dislodged us from a lot of stuck patterns, opened up new worlds for us, let us breathe different air. A couple of years on, living on the water on the edge of a suburb feels entirely normal.

Even better, moving out of East Vancouver is recalibrating my colonized ideas of home and place and fixity. I used to talk about "our" neighborhood, deploying the grammars and politics of "community" to justify my place there, and my right to speak of and for it. I believed that East Vancouver was my home, my place to defend as my own. I feel embarrassed about that now. It is the same language that the National Front and Tucker Carlson and every other anti-immigration, racist asshole uses to justify their occupation and control of land. I am glad to have shed it, and really hope I have shed it for good.

People have to be able to stay in place over duration. A foundational tenet of anti-colonial, anti-capitalist politics is that people are able to make decisions about their own bodies, where and when they move, and what happens to the land they live on. But those narratives are always clouded by private property and the impositions of colonial settlement, and our family is no different: how we chose to move is a decision we made, but hardly on our own. We had, and have, a lot of choices, but in other senses our field of possibility is highly constrained and wanting.

7

Often, when people speak elegiacally about cities or neighborhoods where they no longer feel welcome or at home, they remark on how everything happened so fast. That change came quicker than they could adjust or respond to, that capital sprints while policy and governance and most of us walk or move at a crawl. Relationships take so long to build but then get scattered just like that.

I'm highly suspicious of all nostalgia. Which were the good old days worth pining for? Back when Black people couldn't vote? Or when husbands could rape their wives, or beat their children? When people died of diseases that now have simple cures? Those days?

Vine Deloria, in his book *God Is Red*, famously differentiated between "American Indian" and "Western European" metaphysics. Deloria claimed that Indigenous people see land as having "the highest possible meaning, and all their statements are made with this reference point in mind," while Western thinking views the world historically in terms of development, and thus there is a fundamental disconnect between those "concerned with the philosophical problem of space" and those primarily interested in "the philosophical problem of time."[8]

Glen Coulthard asserts that this argument goes well beyond banal notions of Indigenous people's so-called mystical attachments to their homelands but rather suggests an

> ontological argument for understanding relationships . . . Place is a way of knowing, of experiencing and relating to the world and with others; and sometimes those relational practices and forms of knowledge guide forms of resistance against other rationalizations of the world that threaten to erase or destroy our senses of place.[9]

I think Coulthard's argument here can inform a renovated relationship with the city and inform resistances and refusals. Often colonialism is described as the theft of space while capitalism is the theft of time, which is fine as a broad-brush description, but we don't have to venture too far into quantum mechanics to describe space and time as constantly entwined, each giving permission to one another. Because they are functionally impossible to separate from one another, space and time have an integral relationship, and spacetime flows differently relative to one's position.

Building on Deloria's ontologically relevant insights, Coulthard urges us to consider how non-oppressive relations are constituted, which we can translate to the urban and ask after the constituent elements of non-oppressive human settlements, but as experienced differently from relative points of view.[10] We can refuse the *urb* or the *sub*, and we can refuse the centering and accumulation functions of domination. We can provincialize colonial centers of empire and we can provincialize any presumptively fixed points of the city that anchor the recursive logics of property. That's a theoretical exercise, but far more is a here-and-now project.

Sitting at a bar together one cold winter afternoon, I asked Deborah Cowen, a professor of geography at the University of Toronto, about how she thinks about the centres of Toronto. She used to live in Parkdale in the 1990s, a classic inner-city neighborhood that is now a flashpoint for anti-gentrification organizing. Located about five kilometers west of the downtown core and including one of the biggest diasporic Tibetan communities in the world, Parkdale has been among the scrappiest and funkiest of Toronto's downtown neighborhoods, hanging on to its distinct flavor even as so many others lost their cheap rental stock and succumbed to waves of displacement.

In many ways Parkdale has been fighting back better than most; it is still a fun place with some brilliant community organizing around renter resistance and community land trusts, but it seems like only a matter of time before the neighborhood is hollowed out of affordable housing stock. It's just too attractive a place, too close to the downtown core and too vulnerable to hold back the tides of capital and investment. Cowen says she could smell it coming even when she lived there, and the neighborhood was a little rough and unpalatable for most.

"I used to say, in a kind of flip way, that I gave up on the inner city years ago," she once told a reporter. "In terms of being homogeneous, predictable, corporate and maybe even securitized —that certainly seems like the fate of Toronto, and without some kind of dramatic change, it will be." Cowen has long argued for swift and forceful progressive municipal action, waged on multiple fronts—taxing speculation, supporting renters, building affordable housing and all the rest. But, she says, even at her most optimistic, "I'm not convinced even that is enough to effect the change we need . . . what kind of city will be left to save?"[11]

Cowen looked off in the middle distance when I asked her what was going to happen to the Toronto neighborhoods she loved. She looked composed, if a little resigned, about the velocities of capital: "People move and make and remake worlds. No one is tied inescapably to one neighborhood or building. It's sad to be forced out, but it's no secret why the most vibrant areas of Toronto are now Scarborough, Brampton and places way off the hipster radar."

It's been said that as soon as movement is stopped, space becomes historical, which is precisely what border policing attempts. Borders, by their nature, efface pluralities, and the fixity of capital property relations attempts the same. Claiming an urban center and then policing what counts and does not count as "urban" abrogates existing social relations, jamming them into a single set of relational possibilities.

I am highly suspicious of the late-capitalist value of "the city" as a meaningful unit of political organizing. But this is far from an easy, unproblematic assertion I am making here. Urban studies has been roiled over the past decades, as people in the field are substantively pissy about what a "city" is—is it a thing? A way of thinking, an ideological formation? Or can we reject the idea of the "city" as something not worth mobilizing around? In *The Urban Revolution*, Henri Lefebvre famously claimed that the "concept of the city no longer corresponds to a social object.

Sociologically it is a pseudoconcept." But he went on to claim that the historical weight of the city leaves it as a representational image that continues to exert profound influence, so much so that urbanism is now completely encompassing.[12]

A wave of contemporary scholars have built out that thesis, most popularly the planetary urbanists who claim that urban theory has become so fragmented and fractured (like cities themselves), without any methodological or political coherence, that "in the early twenty-first century, the urban appears to have become a quintessential floating signifier: devoid of any clear definitional parameters, morphological coherence, or cartographic fixity."[13] In response, they describe the urban form as exploded/imploded and argue for "a new epistemology of the urban," an urbanization without end.

You already know my thinking on this: the work of planetary urbanism is legitimate and interesting, and worthy of sustained and respectful engagement as a radical intervention. It's not the place here to relitigate a debate that has turned into a volatile and painful brawl, but I can accept the idea of the city as a historical form of life, a concept, a way of being in the world. However, the explosion of the city into *urban*, *suburban*, *post-urban* and a million other variants does not warrant its re-inscription as a theoretical ordering mechanism.

To try and muscle the "city" into a fixed and totalizing concept is not a descriptive approach; it is a prescriptive, regulating and governing mechanism. The fear of messiness, of incoherence, of fracturing or fragmentation is worth resisting constantly. This is precisely the work that so many postcolonial theorists have spent so much time and energy beautifully articulating, and is precisely what I encounter when I try and get sophisticated downtown urbanites to come to Surrey. Even among dear friends, people with great politics, people who know they should know better, the revulsion is palpable at having to come to the sub-urbs, the sprawling, incoherent mess that is Surrey.

I have to beg people to come, have to offer to come and pick them up and drive them out here, reassure them that it really is safe and that there really are coffee shops (okay, fine, they're all chains, but still.) As soon as you enter Surrey, the concept of the urban starts to fray and disorient every bourgeois claim to the city. I know the feeling because I was that guy, and in some respects am still fighting that tendency—forcing this place into a nostalgic and constraining rendition of what a city should be.

Instead, I want urban studies and urban organizing to be far more generous and open-hearted, to be able to see the sub-urbs for real, not as some extension or perversion or weak replication of the *urb*, but as vibrant places of refusal and creativity. I think David Wachsmuth is essentially right when he argues that "we should neither dismiss the concept of the city as outdated nor try to resuscitate it as a category of analysis, but rather treat it as a category of practice, a representation of urbanization processes that exceed it."[14] That's not bad but tries to split the baby too cautiously. Why try so hard? I like Natalie Oswin's formulation so much more: "Yes, capitalism is everywhere. But so is everything else. And there are outsides—constitutive ones—all over the place."[15] This is perfect. There really are outsides everywhere, all over the place—so many, actually, that it makes no sense to call them outside. They are not *outside* of anything.

8

I hope you have not read this book as an argument to abandon your inner-city neighborhoods and rush to occupy the sub-urbs. I hope you have read it as an argument for pluriversalities, especially in urban thinking and organizing. I hope you have read it as an attempt to mess with any fixed ideas about what the city is or should be.

It only takes a few minutes on the outside to see how fragile and paternalistic and thin most so-called progressive urbanist thinking is, and how quickly the arrogant notions of so much of contemporary urban studies fall apart. You can see how easily the weight of whiteness bends the arc of city thinking, but also how easily new versions can come into view.

Consider the case of Senáḵw, a new housing development being built by the *Sḵwx̱wú7mesh Úxwumixw* (Squamish Nation) right in the heart of Vancouver, at the head of False Creek in the idyllic neighborhood of Kitsilano. Senáḵw was a traditional village site, used since long before recorded history by Sḵwx̱wú7mesh people who traveled there seasonally to hunt, fish and gather resources. The area was under assault soon after European contact and was first expropriated for railways in the late 1800s. Then settlers illegally seized the village site itself, selling off parcels for all kinds of purposes, including as an armory, training site and equipment depot, while Sḵwx̱wú7mesh people were relocated and contained in twenty-three separate reserves scattered across Metro Vancouver and up the Howe Sound. In 2003 the Federal Court of Canada finally returned Senáḵw to Squamish Nation control, granting them a misshapen 10.48-acre portion of the original 80 acres.

SEEING LIKE A SUB-URB

The site is now in a prime central location in the city, and the Sḵwx̱wú7mesh Úxwumixw and their development arm (the Nch'ḵaẏ Development Corporation) are building a hugely ambitious eleven tower, four million-square-foot mixed-use development that is going to create more than six thousand rental units, including twelve hundred affordable units. It will be the largest net-zero-carbon residential project in the country and the largest First Nations economic development project in Canadian history.

The initial plans that have been released for Senáḵw are amazing—they look Wakanda-esque, merging futuristic, techno-logically sophisticated architecture with Sḵwx̱wú7mesh design principles. It is also going to create Hong Kong–levels of density, with the tallest towers planned at fifty-six stories, relying heavily on transit access, bike lanes and pedestrian-friendly design. And because the land is not municipal—it is federal reserve land, with the Sḵwx̱wú7mesh Úxwumixw granted authority—the developers can skip past the tangle of city permitting and licensing bureaucracies and are planning to complete the first phases in as little as five years from outset.

It is an unusual, maybe unprecedented, development in many ways, in part because it is uncommon for an Indigenous nation to have such prime inner-city land under control. As Ginger Gosnell-Myers, who served from 2013 to 2018 as Vancouver's first Indigenous relations manager, notes, the Canadian reserve system was designed to push Indigenous people well to the outside: "If you look at where reserves have been placed in this country, they're largely on the outskirts. That's by design . . . We're looking at a deliberate history of exclusion."[16]

And, of course, there is now significant and accelerating pushback coming from local white residents, politicians and pundits, including many of the city's most prominent expo-nents of "sustainable urbanism." They are dredging up every predictably laughable objection: the density is going to be inconsistent with the precious neighborhood around it; it will overwhelm the aesthetics of the nearby Burrard Bridge;[17] there is not enough integration into the transit infrastructure;[18] there hasn't been enough consultation;[19] the development will drive a three-hundred-meter road through the existing parkland.[20] One of the most cringeworthy of the neighborhood groups, No Road Through Vanier Park,[21] who has been rallying the opposition, is taking the city to court to try to stop the development.[22] Jeremy Braude, a retired local resident who is leading the charge, put it more frankly: "You start to worry about what's happening in your backyard and frankly, this is my backyard and it's also the people of Canada's backyard. This is a federal park. Why does the federal government have to give it away for no good reason?"[23] Several city councilors past and present have suggested that Vancouver's so-called livability, a.k.a. its "Vancouverism," is at risk if not enough concessions are extracted from the project.[24]

Senákw is almost certainly going to be built, and the opposition has to be read as another round of racist attempts to deny Indigenous people access to their land and resources. Given the history of Indigenous people's violent expulsion from these same lands, the irony of white settlers begging for this project to slow down and consult more thoroughly is a bit thick. Everyone loves density and billion-dollar investments and innovation until the Indigenous people move back in.

It is a transformative project to be sure, but it's more than that: Senákw points to a renovated idea of what cities can be, and the incredible creativity that is possible when cities are permeable and unfixed, if the outside can seep in and seep out. If urbanists can somehow see all the outsides all around us, then the idea of what is the center and what is the periphery starts to dissolve.

This is the mess we can rely on as the most alive source of revolt and refusal and regeneration. If we can learn to think like a sub-urb for a minute, if we can stop constantly ordering settlements based on Lockean propertied ontologies, then real openings emerge for building alternatives to racial capitalism. What some might call the "messy edges" are where it is most possible to avoid the capture of planning. As Lefebvre wrote almost fifty years ago now:

Pressure from below must therefore also confront the state in its role as organiser of space, as the power that controls urbanization, the construction of buildings and spatial planning in general. The state defends class interests while simultaneously setting itself above society as a whole, and its ability to intervene in space can and must be turned back against it, by grass-roots opposition, in the form of counter-plans and counter-projects designed to thwart strategies, plans and programmes imposed from above.[25]

As Karl Polanyi once wrote, "Laissez-faire was planned."[26] To escape the confluence of state and capital that frantically works to maintain believable orders, to maintain the rights to profit, to expropriation and exploitation, we have to become illegible to that ordering. The contemporary neoliberal urban form is a machine for profit, expelling those who cannot be efficiently exploited. To refuse, we have to construct believable alternatives, in theory as much as in everyday life.

Theorizing—or figuring out what the hell is going on—has to mean getting outside the outside, refusing the languages of peripheralization that center certain kinds of power and dictate who gets access to resources and mobilities. If we can renovate the way we talk about and see cities, then we'll have a shot at refusing and revolting effectively. If we are going to fight to win, if anti-poverty and racial justice and ecological and abolitionist movements are for real, then we have to stop invoking the same tired tropes and colonizing languages that have built our cities. There are other languages, better ways to conduct ourselves, and more powerful ways to organize all around us.

Acknowledgments

This book took me somewhat longer to complete than I intended. As the pandemic was disheveling all our plans, I used some of that unasked-for extra time to let my thinking sprawl—pun more or less intended. I am very grateful for that lacuna now, as it both clarified and expanded what I thought I was trying to say. More than that, I just had a ton more time to do research—mostly just working and living in Surrey and other suburbs.

I feel proud of this book and where it has arrived, in part because it took me so long to get here. But the effort required even more forbearance and counsel than usual from friends and foes alike. So many people sat and worked through ideas with me, patiently and not. I'm going to miss thanking many of you here—please blame my advancing years for my rudeness—but know I appreciate you and hope you all see something of your wisdom in the book.

The first people to thank are everyone at Verso; specifically Leo Hollis, Nick Walther and Brian Baughan, each of whom laboured long and hard to improve this writing and helped to shape the book significantly. This would have been a much poorer offering without their insights and diligence, so huge thanks to all three and the many folks I have not met at Verso but who have made the book possible.

Second are Ananya Roy and Roger Keil. They are both tremendously accomplished scholars who answered a rando's email, helped me to really see what I was seeing, and were unfailingly kind over the course of many years as they encouraged me to pursue this work. It is not hyperbole to say that this book would not exist without them.

Third are the key people in each place I visited. John Washington, Loretta Lees, Max Rousseau and Maryame Amarouche all appear prominently in the book, and they were essential to my thinking, but I leaned on many other people in Portland, Rabat, London, St. Louis and other cities that did not make it in here. They include: Ashley Dornan, Shane Trudell, Geoff Mann, Neil Brenner, Fulong Wu, Deb Cowen, Olusola Olabiyi, Dave Carter, Franci Duran, Leslie Wood, Jamal Williams, Pushpa Arabindoo, Juan Jose Bocanegra, John Fox, Mike D, Theresa C.A., Howard Greenwich, the Hilltop Action Coalition, Scott Allard, Maiko Winkler-Chin, Tim Thomas, Jasmine Jackson, Lisa Bates, Sam Lemil, Fawn Aberson, Nathan McClintock, Karim, Rabie and Ibrahim Mohamed, Houssine, Hamid, Farouk, Lara, M'Barka, Amir Mohammed, Darryl and Shane Amir, Sam Roddick, Brett Story, Julia Ho, Inez Bordeaux, the ArchCity Defenders, Cathy's Kitchen, Carlos Teixeira, and Khelsilem.

Of course, there are several goons who I run most all my ideas past and can always trust for salty critiques: Am Johal, Glen Coulthard, all the Portuguese Club crew, and of course Sadie, Daisy and Selena, who generously and brilliantly let me test-run all of this way too often. More than anyone, though, I'd like to thank my friends and colleagues throughout Surrey, but most especially and always to everyone at Solid State. I don't deserve any of you and am grateful every day for your friendship.

Notes

Part 1

1. James Howard Kunstler, "The Ghastly Tragedy of the Suburbs," TED talk, 2004, ted.com.
2. Roshini Nair and Tara Carman, "East Vancouver Becoming Less Diverse, Census Shows," CBC News, October 28, 2017.
3. Eyal Press, "The New Suburban Poverty," *Nation*, April 13, 2007.
4. "A Planet of Suburbs: Places Apart," *Economist*, December 6, 2014.
5. Elizabeth Kneebone, "Job Sprawl Revisited: The Changing Geography of Metropolitan Employment," Brookings Institution, April 6, 2009.
6. Patrick Sisson, "How the Pandemic Supercharged Sprawl," *Bloomberg CityLab*, January 5, 2022; Creeson Agecoutay and Ross Anderson, "Canadians Leaving Big Cities in Record Numbers: Statistics Canada," CTV News, January 16, 2021; Gabby Birenbaum, "Everyone's Moving to the Suburbs," *Washington Monthly*, November 23, 2020.
7. Elizabeth Kneebone, "The Suburbanization of Poverty: Trends in Metropolitan America, 2000 to 2008," Brookings Institution, January 20, 2010.
8. John Sullivan, "Black America Is Moving South—and to the 'Burbs. What's It Mean?," *ColorLines*, October 10, 2011.
9. Emily Badger, "The Suburbanization of Poverty," *CityLab*, May 20, 2013.
10. William Frey, "Today's Suburbs Are Symbolic of America's Rising Diversity: A 2020 Census Portrait," Brookings Institution, June 15, 2022.
11. Sandhya Dirks, "Suburbs Are Now the Most Diverse Areas in America," *All Things Considered*, NPR, November 8, 2022.
12. William H. Frey, "The Suburbs: Not Just for White People Anymore," *New Republic*, November 24, 2014.
13. Frey, "Today's Suburbs Are Symbolic of America's Rising Diversity."
14. Hugh Muir, "Black Flight: How England's Suburbs Are Changing Colour," *Guardian*, July 8, 2016.
15. Mary O'Hara, "Alan Berube: We Are Moving Poverty to the Suburbs," *Guardian*, May 6, 2015.

16. Jay Caspian Kang, "Everything You Know about the Suburbs Is Wrong," *New York Times*, November 8, 2021.

17. Abhijeet Chavan, "How New Jersey's Levittown Became 70% Black," *Planetizen*, June 28, 2003.

18. "Race and Ethnicity in Maryvale, Phoenix, Arizona," Statistical Atlas, statisticalatlas.com.

19. Mireille Vézina and René Houle, "Settlement Patterns and Social Integration of the Population with an Immigrant Background in the Montréal, Toronto and Vancouver Metropolitan Areas," Statistics Canada, May 8, 2017.

20. Ibid.

21. Carlos Texeira, personal interview, February, 16, 2023.

22. Douglas Todd, "Does Burnaby Have the World's Most 'Super-Diverse' Neighbourhood in the World?," *Vancouver Sun*, November 3, 2015.

23. Elizabeth Kneebone, "The Changing Geography of US Poverty," Brookings Institution, February 15, 2017.

24. Joe Cortright, "Reality Check: Poverty Rates Are Much Lower in the Suburbs," *City Observatory*, December 7, 2017.

25. Elizabeth Kneebone, "Ferguson, MO. Emblematic of Growing Suburban Poverty," *The Avenue* (Brookings Institution blog), August 15, 2014.

26. Alan Ehrenhalt, *The Great Inversion and the Future of the American City* (New York: Vintage Books, 2013), 38.

27. Richard Harris and Robert Lewis, "The Geography of North American Cities and Suburbs," *Journal of Urban History* 27, no. 3 (March 2001): 263.

28. Roger Keil, personal conversation, January 3, 2018.

29. Some of the best post-suburban readings that I have relied on include, in no particular order: J. C. Teaford, *Post-suburbia: Government and Politics in the Edge Cities* (Baltimore: Johns Hopkins University Press, 1997); Nicholas Phelps et al., "A Postsuburban World? An Outline of a Research Agenda," *Environment and Planning A* 42, no. 2 (2010): 366–83; Rob Kling, Spencer Olin, and Mark Poster, eds., *Postsuburban California: The Transformation of Orange County since World War II* (California: University of California Press, 1995); E. W. Soja, *Postmetropolis: Critical Studies of Cities and Regions* (Oxford: Basil Blackwell, 2000); Marco Helbich and Michael Leitner, "Spatial Analysis of the Urban-to-Rural Migration Determinants in the Viennese Metropolitan Area. A Transition from Suburbia to Postsuburbia?" *Applied Spatial Analysis and Policy* 2, no. 3 (2009): 237–60; Robert Musil, "Globalized Post-suburbia," *Belgeo. Revue belge de géographie* 1 (2007) 147–62; Nicholas A. Phelps and Andrew M. Wood, "The New Post-suburban Politics?" *Urban Studies* 48, no. 12 (2011): 2591–610.

30. Eric Charmes and Roger Keil, "The Politics of Post-suburban

Densification in Canada and France," *International Journal of Urban and Regional Research* 39, no. 3 (2015): 581–602.

31. Dennis Romero, "L.A. Is America's "Least Sprawling" City!?," *LA Weekly*, February 18, 2015.

32. Ananya Roy, "Who's Afraid of Postcolonial Theory?," *International Journal of Urban and Regional Research* 40, no. 1 (January 2016): 200–9.

33. Jennifer Robinson, *Ordinary Cities* (London: Routledge, 2005).

34. Many thanks to Rob Nichols for stimulating my thinking on this point. He writes: "Since dispossession presupposes prior *possession*, recourse to it appears conservative and tends to reinforce the very proprietary and commoditized models of social relations that radical critics generally seek to undermine." Robert Nichols, "Theft Is Property! The Recursive Logic of Dispossession," *Political Theory* 46, no. 1 (2018): 3–28.

35. Matt Hern, *What a City Is For: Remaking the Politics of Displacement* (Cambridge, MA: MIT Press, 2016).

36. Jamie Peck, "Neoliberal Suburbanism: Frontier Space," *Urban Geography* 32, no. 6 (2011): 885–6.

37. Ibid., 885.

38. Oliver Milman, "Right-Wing Climate Denial Is Being Replaced—by Nativism," *Mother Jones*, November 22, 2021.

39. Tucker Carlson, "Tucker Carlson Responds to His Immigration Critics: We're Not Intimidated and Will Continue to Tell the Truth," Fox News, December 18, 2018.

40. James C. Scott, *The Art of Not Being Governed: An Anarchist History of Upland Southeast Asia* (New Haven: Yale University Press, 2009).

41. Doug Brown, "A Black Teen Was Run Down in Gresham," *Portland Mercury*, August 31, 2016.

42. Aaron Scott, "By the Grace of God," *Portland Monthly*, March 2012.

43. Alan Berger, *Drosscapes: Wasting Land in Urban America* (Princeton, NJ: Princeton University Press, 2006).

44. Richard Rothstein, *The Making of Ferguson: Public Policies at the Root of Its Troubles*, Economic Policy Institute, October 2014. This report is a prelude to Rothstein's 2017 book, *The Color of Law: A Forgotten History of How Our Government Segregated America*, which itself is prelude to a 2023 follow-up book called *Just Action: How to Challenge Segregation Enacted under the Color of Law*.

45. Ibid.

46. World Population Review, "St. Louis, Missouri Population 2023," worldpopulationreview.com.

47. National Geospatial-Intelligence Agency, nga.mil.

48. Katie Nodjimbadem, "The Racial Segregation of American Cities Was Anything but Accidental," *Smithsonian Magazine*, May 30, 2017.

49. Ryan Schuessler, "One by One, Missouri's Black Towns Disappear,"

Al Jazeera America, April 5, 2014.

50. Monica Davey, "Panel Studying Racial Divide in Missouri Presents a Blunt Picture of Inequity," *New York Times*, September 14, 2015.

51. The Hill (@thehill), Twitter, July 12, 2020, twitter.com/thehill/status/1282364884211109888.

52. Samuel Sinyangwe, "Police Are Killing Fewer People in Big Cities, but More in Suburban and Rural America," *FiveThirtyEight*, June 1, 2020.

53. ArchCity Defenders, *Death by the State: Police Killings and Jail Deaths in St. Louis*, January 2021. The report cites data from Mapping Police Violence: mappingpoliceviolence.org.

54. Laura Begley Bloom, "Report Ranks America's 15 Safest (and Most Dangerous) Cities for 2023," *Forbes*, January 31, 2023.

55. Timothy Bella, "Missouri Republicans Block Proposed Ban on Kids Carrying Guns in Public," *Washington Post*, February 9, 2023.

56. Timothy Bella, "Missouri Republicans Adopt Stricter House Dress Code—but Just for Women," *Washington Post*, January 12, 2023.

57. Mariame Kaba, "Yes, We Mean Literally Abolish the Police," *New York Times*, op-ed, June 14, 2020.

Part 2

1. Andrew Wiese, *Places of Their Own: African American Suburbanization in the 20th Century* (Chicago: University of Chicago Press, 2004); Charles Abrams, *Forbidden Neighbors: A Study of Prejudice in Housing* (New York: Harper and Brothers, 1955); Kenneth T. Jackson, *Crabgrass Frontier: The Suburbanization of the United States* (New York: Oxford University Press, 1985).

2. H. J. Gans, *The Levittowners: Ways of Life and Politics in a New Suburban Community* (New York: Columbia University Press, 2017); William H. Whyte, *The Organization Man* (Philadelphia: University of Pennsylvania Press, 2013).

3. W. E. B. Du Bois, *Darkwater: Voices from within the Veil* (1921; repr., Millwood, NY: Kraus-Thomson Organization, 1991), chap. 2, 29–30.

4. Aileen Moreton-Robinson, *The White Possessive: Property, Power, and Indigenous Sovereignty* (Minneapolis: University of Minnesota Press, 2015), xi.

5. Ibid., xii, xix.

6. Cheryl Harris, "Whiteness as Property," *Harvard Law Review* 106, no. 8 (1993): 1707.

7. Moreton-Robinson, *The White Possessive*, xix.

8. Lorenzo Veracini, "Suburbia, Settler Colonialism and the World Turned Inside Out," *Housing, Theory and Society* 29, no. 4 (2012): 339–57.

9. Ibid., 352.

10. Elizabeth Becker, "2 Farm Acres Lost Per Minute, Study Says," *New York Times*, October 4, 2002; Dan Nosowitz, "10 Numbers That Show How Much Farmland We Are Losing to Development," *Modern Farmer*, May 22, 2018.

11. Rajyashree Reddy, "The Urban under Erasure: Towards a Postcolonial Critique of Planetary Urbanization," *Environment and Planning D: Society and Space* 36, no. 3 (2018): 529–39.

12. Pretty much anything insightful in this chapter is heavily reliant on Maryame's and Max's support and guidance. They helped me patiently, read many drafts and kindly directed me. Any errors here are all mine for sure: they could weed out most of my mistakes, but not all. They are tremendous scholars.

13. Elli Thomas, Ilona Serwicka, and Paul Swinney, *Urban Demographics: Where People Live and Work*, Centre for Cities, July 2015.

14. Fiona Simpson, "Tooting Named One of 10 Coolest Neighbourhoods on Earth by Lonely Planet," *Evening Standard*, August 24, 2017.

15. Richard Florida, "Class-Divided Cities: London Edition," *Bloomberg CityLab*, November 5, 2013.

16. Loretta Lees, "The Geography of Gentrification: Thinking through Comparative Urbanism," *Progress in Human Geography* 36, no. 2 (2012): 144–71.

17. Hagar Kotef, *Movement and Ordering of Freedom: On Liberal Governances of Mobility* (Durham, NC: Duke University Press, 2015), 5.

18. Alexander Follmann et al., "Peri-urban Transformation in the Global South: A Comparative Socio-spatial Analytics Approach," *Regional Studies* (2022): 1–15.

Part 3

1. Ali Pitargue, "What's the History of the Brentwood College Site? How Mill Bay Became Home to B.C.'s First Children's Hospital," *Discourse*, June 16, 2020.

2. Kotef, *Movement and Ordering of Freedom*, 4–5.

3. Glen Coulthard, *Red Skins, White Masks: Rejecting the Colonial Politics of Recognition* (Minneapolis: University of Minnesota Press, 2014), 78.

4. David Wengrow and David Graeber, *The Dawn of Everything: A New History of Humanity* (London: Allen Lane, 2021), 276–327.

5. Daisy Couture et al., *On This Patch of Grass: City Parks on Occupied Land* (Halifax, Canada: Fernwood Publishing, 2019).

6. Helena Hanson, "Canada's Most Dangerous Cities Have Been Ranked & They're Not Where You'd Expect," Narcity, October 5, 2022.

7. Numbeo, "Current Crime Index," 2023, numbeo.com.

8. Vine Deloria, *God Is Red* (New York: Grossett and Dunlap, 1973), 61–3.

9. Coulthard, *Red Skins, White Masks*, 63.

10. Ibid., 62.

11. Murray Whyte, "'My Parkdale Is Gone': How Gentrification Reached the One Place That Seemed Immune," *Guardian*, January 14, 2020.

12. Henri Lefebvre, *The Urban Revolution* (Minnesota: University of Minnesota Press, 2003), 57.

13. Neil Brenner, "Theses on Urbanization," *Public Culture* 25, no. 1 (2013): 90.

14. David Wachsmuth, "City as Ideology: Reconciling the Explosion of the City Form with the Tenacity of the City Concept," *Environment and Planning D: Society and Space* 32, no. 1 (2014): 76.

15. Natalie Oswin, "Planetary Urbanization: A View from Outside," *Environment and Planning D: Society and Space* 36, no. 3 (2016): 5.

16. Matthew Halliday, "The Bold New Plan for an Indigenous-Led Development in Vancouver," *Guardian*, January 3, 2020.

17. Ben Miljure, "Kitsilano Residents Still Trying to Stop Access Road for Senakw Development," CTV News Vancouver, September 7, 2022.

18. Francis Bula, "Squamish Nation Development in Vancouver Aims to Add 10,000 Residents, Creating the City's Densest Community Yet," *Globe and Mail*, August 13, 2022.

19. Douglas Todd, "Why Is Vancouver So Secretive about this First Nations' Highrise Project?," *Vancouver Sun*, July 27, 2022.

20. Miljure, "Kitsilano Residents Still Trying to Stop Access Road."

21. No Vanier Park Road website, nosenakwroadway.com/index.htm.

22. Maria Weisgarber, "Residents Group Takes Vancouver to Court over Services Agreement for Squamish Nation Development," CTV News, October 6, 2022.

23. Miljure, "Kitsilano Residents."

24. Gordon Price, "Vancouverism Should Cut Both Ways for City, Squamish Nation," *Vancouver Sun*, November 19, 2019.

25. Henri Lefebvre, *The Production of Space* (Oxford: Anthropos, 1974), 382–3.

26. Karl Polanyi, *The Great Transformation: The Political and Economic Origins of Our Time* (New York: Farrar and Rinehart, 1944).

Index

"My good friend Douglas Groothuis is a person of rigorous intellectual depth, integrity, and character forged on the anvil of suffering and Christlike courage to speak truth when it is not popular to do so. *Fire in the Streets* brings all these things together. The result is a careful, intellectually informed, heartfelt, and bold treatment of a range of social, ethical, and political topics that constitute today's chaotic culture. When you read this book, be prepared for hard-hitting straight talk backed up with carefully crafted arguments. If you don't agree with his claims, then provide reasons why he is wrong."

    —J. P. Moreland, professor of philosophy at Biola University
       and contributor to *Dissident Philosophers: Voices against*
       the Political Current of the Academy

"*Fire in the Streets* is a timely and eye-opening book. Groothuis offers a biblical and philosophical critique of Critical Race Theory that Christians—whether they agree with his assessment or not—need to take seriously. This book deserves to be read, analyzed, and discussed widely."

    —Sean McDowell, professor of apologetics at Biola
       University, speaker, and author

"*Fire in the Streets* is wise Christian counsel to Americans who are concerned about the rise of Critical Race Theory and its equally destructive kindred ideologies. CRT, the fire that is currently burning in our streets, has been subject to many other critiques, but Groothuis brings something new to the table. He seeks to fight that destructive cultural fire with the 'good fire' of 'well-reasoned, knowledgeable, and humble conviction that the American creed is worth reaffirming and living.' His argument is meticulous, respectful, and frequently eloquent."

    —Peter W. Wood, president of the National Association of
       Scholars and author of *1620: A Critical Response to the*
       1619 Project

"What are Christians to do in our present American age? Too many Christians are not equipped by their churches to properly engage the most pressing issues of our time. How does the Bible guide us in the public square? Dr. Doug Groothuis brilliantly explores these issues with a foundation on Christ's mandate to serve each other with the love of God. Grace and Truth are critical for America to continue. This is must-read for every Christian."

  —**Jeff Hunt,** director of Centennial Institute at Colorado Christian University

FIRE IN THE STREETS

FIRE
IN THE
STREETS

How You Can Confidently Respond to Incendiary Cultural Topics

DOUGLAS R. GROOTHUIS

SALEM
BOOKS
an imprint of Regnery Publishing
Washington, D.C.

Salem Books™ is a trademark of Salem Communications Holding Corporation. Regnery® is a registered trademark and its colophon is a trademark of Salem Communications Holding Corporation.

ISBN: 978-1-68451-308-6
eISBN: 978-1-68451-317-8
Library of Congress Control Number: 2022937279

Published in the United States by
Salem Books
An Imprint of Regnery Publishing
A Division of Salem Media Group
Washington, D.C.
www.SalemBooks.com

Manufactured in the United States of America

10 9 8 7 6 5 4 3 2 1

Books are available in quantity for promotional or premium use. For information on discounts and terms, please visit our website: www.SalemBooks.com.